SO YOU WANT TO BE A GREAT VOLLEYBALL COACH

TOD MATTOX

THEARTOFCOACHINGVOLLEYBALL.COM

Copyright © 2021 Total Sports, LLC

All rights reserved. This book or any portion thereof may not be reproduced or used in any manner whatsoever without the express written permission of the publisher except for the use of brief quotations in a book review.

Printed in the United States of America

First Printing, June 2021

ISBN: 978-1-7347652-4-3

Written by Tod Mattox
Edited by Don Patterson

Published by Total Sports, LLC
322 Encinitas Boulevard, Suite 280
Encinitas, CA 92024

www.theartofcoachingvolleyball.com

TABLE OF CONTENTS

Part 1: Where Do I Begin?
Tip 1: Put First Things First   **1**
Tip 2: Build a Strong Foundation, Part I – Purpose and Vision   **2**
Tip 3: Build a Strong Foundation, Part II – Values and Culture   **5**
Tip 4: Learn the Fundamentals of Coaching (Basic Maxims)   **7**
Tip 5: Expand Your Volleyball Vocabulary   **11**
Tip 6: Know the Rules   **15**

Part 2: How Do I Start My Team?
Tip 7: Determine Your Team's Level   **21**
Tip 8: Tryouts, Part I – Align Your Team Size with Your Goals   **23**
Tip 9: Tryouts, Part II – Make Your First Impression a Great One   **26**
Tip 10: Establish Standards of Behavior   **29**
Tip 11: Hone Your Communication Skills (Part I) – Employ the Rules of 3, 10 and 30   **31**
Tip 12: Hone Your Communication Skills (Part II) – Praise in Public and Correct in Public   **33**
Tip 13: Hone Your Communication Skills (Part III) – Use Guided Discovery   **35**
Tip 14: Coach Parents, Too   **37**
Tip 15: Use Captains to Reinforce Your Culture   **39**

Part 3: How Do I Teach the Skills?
Tip 16: Use Key Words to Chunk Information   **43**
Tip 17: Start with Movement   **45**
Tip 18: Integrate Reading into Every Skill You Teach   **47**
Tip 19: Teach Attacking First   **49**
Tip 20: Become a Topspin Expert   **52**

Tip 21: Know the Key to Teaching Attacker Timing	**54**
Tip 22: Combine Passing and Serve-receive Training	**56**
Tip 23: Teach Serve-receive Passing with K-I-S-S	**58**
Tip 24: For Serving, Remember to Teach Tempo	**59**
Tip 25: Teach the Jump Float, Early and Often	**62**
Tip 26: When Teaching Setting, Assign Homework	**63**
Tip 27: Teach Passing and Platform (Bump) Setting as Two Distinct Skills	**66**
Tip 28: Combine Forearm and Overhead Digging	**67**
Tip 29: Don't Teach Blocking	**69**
Tip 30: Once You're Ready, Teach Blocking as a Defensive Progression	**71**

Part 4: How Do I Design an Effective Practice?

Tip 31: Begin with Big Picture Planning	**75**
Tip 32: Establish Appropriate Priorities for Your Level	**77**
Tip 33: Wisely Use Your Warm-up Time	**80**
Tip 34: Communicate a Clear End to Each Activity	**82**
Tip 35: Balance Routine with Variety	**84**
Tip 36: When Possible, Turn Drills into Games	**86**
Tip 37: Become an MC (Master of Constraints)	**88**
Tip 38: Use Half-and-half Drills to Set High Standards	**90**
Tip 39: Put Your Assistant(s) to Work	**91**
Tip 40: Remember the F-Words	**94**

Part 5: What's a System, and How Many Do I Need?

Tip 41: Remember Robin Sharma	**97**
Tip 42: Choose System Evolution Over Plug and Play	**99**
Tip 43: Delay Specialization	**101**
Tip 44: Begin at the Beginning – Serve and Serve-receive	**103**
Tip 45: Find Some Setters and Put Them in Middle Front	**106**
Tip 46: Detour – Teach Your Players About Attacking Efficiency	**108**

Tip 47: Detour #2 – Also Teach Them About the Fallacy of Statistics	**110**
Tip 48: On Offense, Set Your Most Efficient Attackers	**112**
Tip 49: Use Common Sense to Position Your Defenders	**114**
Tip 50: Don't Forget About Coverage	**118**
Tip 51: Steal My Favorite System for Developing Teams	**120**

Part 6: What Do I Do During a Match?

Tip 52: Plan Ahead	**123**
Tip 53: Know Your Greatest Challenge	**131**
Tip 54: Sub for Success	**132**
Tip 55: Determine What's Important and Stat It	**135**
Tip 56: Stay Out of the Past	**136**
Tip 57: Be a Gracious Winner and a Grateful Loser	**138**
Tip 58: Learn from My Post-match Debacle	**140**
Tip 59: Find a Couple of Idiots	**142**
Tip 60: Sharpen Your Eavesdropping Skills	**144**
Tip 61: Keep Your Eye Off the Ball	**145**
Tip 62: Stay Curious	**147**

PART 1:
WHERE DO I BEGIN?

TIP 1: PUT FIRST THINGS FIRST

Congrats! You passed the first coaching test. You put first things first.

Let me explain. The best coaches in every sport share one critical trait; they are curious. These coaches are always looking to improve, to gain that little edge that may be the difference between winning and losing. They possess a learner's mindset, and given that you are reading this book, you are in the club. Well done!

This is great news; the fastest way for any team to improve is for the coach to improve. If a coach improves by just a little, the resulting ripple effect from that coach's interactions with each player on the team is a huge multiplier. My intention is that this book will not only help you become better, but more importantly, it will help your team improve.

Though my primary audience for this book is inexperienced coaches who generally work with less experienced players, I'm hopeful that even grizzled veterans coaching the most talented groups can glean some value from these pages. Each of the 62 tips has been useful for me in almost 40 years of coaching. For the majority of my career, I have coached both a beginners' group of middle school girls and high school girls' and boys' varsity teams with several aspiring collegiate players. The tips are applicable from the beginning level to the more advanced.

Feel free to read the book cover to cover, or poke around to the tips that most interest you. Each one is crafted to stand alone as well as be integral to the whole text. Thanks for joining me. Let's get to it!

TIP 2: BUILD A STRONG FOUNDATION, PART I – PURPOSE AND VISION

Everyone would agree that building a house without a proper foundation is a recipe for disaster. Even though a rootless house can be built in record time, and even though it looks like a perfectly fine structure, we know that when foul weather or natural disasters strike, the result will be a pile of rubble.

The same concept applies to teams. As a young coach, I learned this lesson the hard way. Like many who transition from the court to the bench, I was intense, hard-working and hyper-competitive. Early in the season, my efforts often paid dividends. My teams would take pride in their improvement, practicing and competing with energy and enthusiasm.

Unfortunately, the honeymoon wouldn't last. What happened when natural disaster struck in the form of a bad loss, a key injury or a team chemistry issue? You got it. The team crumbled into a pile of rubble because our weak foundation consisted primarily of my need to win. And that wasn't even the worst part. Now, all of my intensity turned to negative energy and became a liability instead of an asset. It was akin to throwing lighter fluid and a match on the debris and watching the resulting inferno.

Please learn from my mistakes and take the time to build a sturdy foundation. Rather than using rebar and concrete, you must employ purpose and vision. Purpose is simply your "Why?" or your reason for coaching. Vision is the ideal future outcome. John Kessel, the former USA Volleyball coaching education guru and a wonderful coaching mentor for me, is a team-building wizard. His purpose and vision are simple and clear. His purpose is to *Grow Leaders*, and his vision is to *Never be a player's last coach*.

For John, when disaster strikes, the foundation is strong. Instead of destroying his team, the process of tackling adversity actually makes the team stronger. Because he is developing leadership, the adversity is never a surprise; it's a necessary part of his leadership curriculum.

For me, my background as a high school English teacher influenced the development of my coaching purpose and vision. My purpose is to *Teach life lessons through volleyball,* and my vision is to *Create a program that players are eager to join, sorry to leave, and that inspires them to give back.*

As a more experienced coach, I can now rely on this foundation to guide me through the inevitable challenges that all coaches face. Whether it's a devastating loss to a weaker opponent or an angry, irrational parent, I have forged a strong philosophical base, and my "house" is now built to last. Furthermore, instead of measuring success in wins and losses, I am more inclined to look at the number of ex-players who find fulfillment through coaching volleyball.

My vision and purpose have evolved over a number of years, but any coach can immediately begin the process. All you need is Google and the coaching staple of "beg, borrow, and steal." That is, if you are a coach for a school or club, you can simply adopt their foundational philosophy. As a high school coach, I can see that the foundational language of the NFHS (National Federation of High Schools) includes: *Promoting respect, integrity, and sportsmanship; Preparing for a future in the global community; Developing leadership and life skills while encouraging a healthy lifestyle.* You can easily find mission statements for colleges on their athletic department websites. A few examples include Harvard's *"Education through Athletics"* and Penn State's *"Preparing students for a lifetime of impact."*

When you find something you like, you may need to tweak it a bit so it relates more to coaching 10-year-old girls than college athletes. Perhaps your purpose is as simple as *"Creating a safe, fun place for my daughter and her friends,"* and your vision is *"Players will love team sports."* Whatever you decide, taking the time to build a solid philosophical foundation will save you countless hours (and heartaches) in the long run.

TIP 3: BUILD A STRONG FOUNDATION, PART II – VALUES AND CULTURE

After purpose and vision, the second column in the foundation is your team's values. For me, purpose and vision help guide the coaches while values guide every individual in the program, especially the players. Identifying team values is a critical first step in the development of your team culture.

Culture is a popular topic in all current team building literature, both in sports and in business. There are countless great models to emulate. As a basketball fan, I love following programs that consistently overachieve. Butler University men's program has sustained mid-major success for over 20 years. Though the school has employed a number of different coaches, the program's values (The Butler Way) have remained the same throughout the turnover in leadership. The Butler Way consists of five pillars: *Humility, Passion, Unity, Servanthood and Gratitude.*

Urban Meyer recently joined the NFL coaching ranks after successful stints at Bowling Green, Utah, Florida and Ohio State. His three core values are: *Relentless Effort, Competitive Excellence and Power of the Unit.* Of course, it's easy to name values and talk about their importance. The magic, however, is integrating the values into your team's daily routine.

Early in my coaching career, I identified three values that were important to me, and these have remained consistent for over 30 years. We limit the number to three because I want them to be "sticky." That is, I want players to remember them easily and live them each and every day. Our three core values are: *Effort, Teamness and Attitude* (ETA). We also put this into a simple equation – ETA = Fun. If every player and coach habitually give maximum effort, if they put the team's success before their own, and if they are consistently positive, we will have a blast!

Our players hear about ETA <u>every day</u>. We begin each practice with a quotation on the whiteboard, and it is always associated with one of our core values. Early in the season, I choose the quotations, and then players select them in the second half of the season. This routine is set in stone; each day we begin with a core value reminder.

During practice, we are also core value-focused. Anytime I choose to stop play to give feedback, I signify its importance by applying it to our core values. If an error is not connected to our core values, I will give "feedback on the fly" and not stop the flow of practice. Examples of times I intervene include:

- Defender doesn't pursue a ball (*Effort*)
- Player stands around while her teammates shag (*Teamness*)
- Player complains about how hot it is in the gym (*Attitude*)

We have also integrated ETA into our end-of-match routine. Win or lose, we gather as a group and share specific examples of ETA that players exhibited during the match. Each player has a turn to share, and then each coach does as well. Rather than celebrate the dramatic (and obvious) straight down hit or stuff block, we make a big deal of celebrating a sub's high energy on the bench, or a DS's cover play. As head coach, I close the meeting, and I'm always looking to highlight an example of selflessness, especially when it's displayed by someone who didn't play a lot. The goal of the meeting is to reinforce our values, and I am always inspired when players recognize their teammates' subtle though critical contributions to our culture.

In that same vein, I regularly remind the team that starters have a much easier role than subs. The starters get plenty of playing time, and they often have a "long leash." If a starter makes a single error, I rarely yank her. On the other hand, a sub often enters the match in critical times when things aren't going well. She must perform, and a single error can often mark the end of her opportunity. As head coach, I have to take the lead when it comes to valuing the contributions of every player, especially the ones who do not receive the strong reinforcement provided by significant playing time. One of my favorite whiteboard quotes is, "You evaluate a team's culture by the behavior of the players on the bench."

To choose your program's values, don't be afraid to beg, borrow and steal from others. However, remember that whichever values you choose become the critical building blocks of your team's culture. Your commitment to reinforcing these may be the most important part of your job as a coach.

TIP 4: LEARN THE FUNDAMENTALS OF COACHING (BASIC MAXIMS)

I'm going to save you a bit of time here. My coaching library is large, and I have spent countless hours reading coaching books. I've condensed it here into eight coaching maxims.

1. **Be a positive role model:** As the leader, your players will naturally look up to you. Your character and work ethic are on display, and players will notice EVERYTHING. Are you on time or late? Make commitments or excuses? Admit mistakes or blame others? Treat refs and opponents with respect or disdain? Lose with grace or resentment? Your team will undoubtedly reflect your behaviors; be sure they are positive ones.

2. **Build strong relationships:** Establishing trusting relationships is critical. Teddy Roosevelt's famous quote is a powerful one for coaches. "Nobody cares how much you know until they know how much you care." Some people are natural relationship-builders, but others (me!) need help. Immediately learning names is a start. Since I have never been the chatty sort, I use a player questionnaire that reveals all kinds of information, from siblings to academic interests to music tastes. This information not only allows me to use relevant, personal analogies when I teach, it also helps an old, slightly senile guy better connect with a Gen Z teenager.

3. **Be organized:** If you teach all day and race out to coach at 3 p.m., there is no worse feeling than scrambling to formulate some kind of plan as you walk in the gym. Taking 10 minutes at lunch to scribble out a plan is a start, but setting aside 20-30 minutes on Sunday night to make a plan for the week is even better.

   Though organization starts with practice planning, it doesn't end there. Communicating with players and their families in advance is another critical component of your organization plan. Disorganized and inconsistent communication is one of the quickest ways to lose credibility with both players and their families.

4. **Prioritize:** Though prioritizing is part of organization, it's important enough to warrant a separate line item. Coaching a beginning volleyball team can be daunting. Often, players can't perform any of the skills. Savvy coaches don't panic when there are only three practices before the first match. They prioritize serving and ace prevention, and when the match arrives, the team quickly learns the importance of those two priorities. The inexperienced coach spends half of the practice time working on setting and spiking, only to discover that their team set and spiked the ball only once in the entire match. Successful prioritizing is most obvious at the beginning level, but it's just as important for all teams, even the most talented.

5. **Be positive:** Given that volleyball skills are difficult to learn and master, it's easy to identify mistakes. It's far more difficult to attain a 5:1 ratio of positive to negative feedback that the Positive Coaching Alliance espouses. This has been a significant challenge for an old error-corrector like me, but I have learned some strategies over the years.

- The first is to remember that any positive contact (hello, good-bye, what's up) can figure into the positive tally.
- The second is instead of pointing out an error, I now catch a player doing it right, and tell everyone to copy it.
- The third is that any positive emotion I communicate should be stronger than any negative emotion. I can be

disappointed when we don't show effort in pursuing a ball, but when we make a great pursuit play, my excitement level has to exceed that previous disappointment level.
- Finally, my goal is to laugh at least three times in every practice.
- Though these may not have pushed me all the way to 5:1, I'm a heck of a lot closer than I was 20 years ago.

6. **Make it fast:** One of my pet peeves is when I see talented young athletes standing around during a volleyball practice. If we want to engage and retain our best athletes, it's important that they have numerous opportunities to display their athleticism. If we don't create these opportunities, they'll run off to soccer and basketball, and we'll be left with a group that loves to stand around. This is especially challenging for coaches of beginning teams, since serving and ace prevention (top priorities for beginners) do not require a lot of movement. We'll get into specific solutions later on in the drill design section; for now, know that our goal is always to keep players moving and learning – less talk and more action.

7. **Make it fun:** Smile, laugh, share your love of the game. One of the reasons volleyball is such a cool sport is its cooperative nature. One player can't grab the ball, weave through a gauntlet of inferior opponents and score. With the exception of an ace serve, it takes a community effort. It is also a sport where even the biggest, baddest players in the world run to the middle of the court to hug after each point. How cool is that! We should relish the opportunity to coach such a fun sport.

8. **Be a great learner:** Improve yourself; improve your team. If you expect your players to get better, then you should be getting better as well. Though I mentioned this in Tip #1, it bears repeating. It's that important.

TIP 5: EXPAND YOUR VOLLEYBALL VOCABULARY

As in any profession, volleyball coaches share a common language. Here are some terms to get you started.

<u>**Areas of the court**</u>**:** There are a couple of ways that coaches identify parts of the court. The first is by location; **LF**, **MF** and **RF** designate left front, middle front and right front. The three back row areas are **LB, MB** and **RB**. Always identify left and right as if you are facing the net. Coaches also assign numbers to each of the six areas. **Area 1** is RB, and the numbers move counterclockwise, so **Area 2** is RF, **3** is MF, **4** is LF, **5** is LB, and **Area 6** is MB. When you see coaches signaling serve locations to their players, they are often using this numerical system.

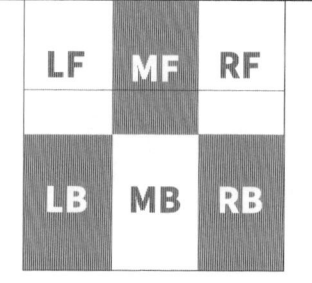
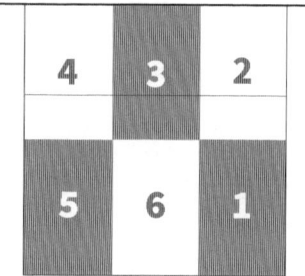

Skills: In the old days, they used to call it "bumping," but that term is out of style. Now, contacting the ball with your **platform** (arms together and extended) is **passing.** There is **serve-receive passing** (often **SR**) and **free ball passing**. Most SR passing is done with the forearms/platform, though overhead passing is legal. **Overhead passing** is taking the first ball with your hands above your head, and it's distinguished from **setting** because a set is a second contact that is fed to an attacker.

A **free ball** is one that the other team either passes or sets over the net, rather than jumping and attacking. The "free" implies that it should be an easy opportunity, and it often is. Of course, I always remember when my team doesn't make it easy. A **down ball** is usually a bit tougher than a free ball, and it is characterized by an attacker who stays "down" and doesn't jump. At the low levels, free and down balls are common. As the level moves up, coaches are not huge fans of giving free and down balls to opponents. They expect an accurate pass to the setter and then a set to an attacker who takes an approach, max jumps and hits/attacks the ball – hard and in, hopefully. In the old days, it was "spike" and "spiker," but now it's usually "attack" and "attacker," though sometimes it's "hit" and "hitter."

An **approach** is the footwork that attackers use to prepare to attack; 3-step and 4-step approaches are most common. More on those later. Attackers don't always hit hard; they can hit offspeed, such as a tip ("dink" in the old days) or roll shot. A **tip** is a one-handed set-like contact that is softly lifted over the block. A **roll shot** looks like a hard attack, but the attacker hits it softly with topspin over the block and into the (hopefully unoccupied) center of the court. Attackers can also **tool**

the block – that is, hit the ball off the block and out of bounds. Most attacks occur on the outside (left side) of the court since almost all setters face the left when they set. Setters can also backset to the right side. A **slide** is usually a right-side backset that an attacker hits with a different approach. Rather than jumping off two feet, the attacker jumps off one leg as you would for a basketball layup. Finally, a **quick attack** or a "**1**" is a fast, low set usually in the middle of the court.

A **serve** starts a point, and the most common types are a **standing float** and a jump float. The float concept resembles a knuckleball in baseball. If the ball is struck with no spin, it will float and move erratically, making it difficult to pass. A standing float is self-explanatory, and for a **jump float**, the server takes a short approach before serving. In men's volleyball, the **jump spin** is most common. For this, the server will self-toss a high set, take a long approach, jump from behind the end-line, and hit the crap out of it. **Blocking** involves jumping at the net to stop or slow down an attack. A **stuff block** lands on the opponent's side and scores a point; a **controlled** or **soft block** slows down an attack so a defender can dig it. In **traditional blocking**, blockers' shoulders usually stay parallel to the net. **Swing blocking** is a more complex and more athletic move. It requires blockers to turn their shoulders perpendicular to the net, then swing their arms like an attacker before jumping to block. On offense after the ball is set, players will **cover** a hitter, which means they gather around to prevent a block from landing on the floor.

<u>**Positions and offensive systems**</u>**:** As players become more accomplished, they are usually put into specialized positions. The most common are **Outside Hitter (OH), Middle Blocker (MB)** – also called Middle Hitter (MH) or Middle Attacker (MA),

Right Side (RS) – also called Opposite (OPP), **Setter (S)**, **Libero (L)** and **Defensive Specialist (DS)**.

The common offensive systems are named with two numbers. The first is the number of attackers used, and the second is the number of setters. A **4-2** is a common system for young players, and a **5-1** and a **6-2** (back row setters, so the setters become attackers in the front row) are most common for more experienced teams. We will get more into systems in Part 5.

Some random terms you should know:

- **Side-out** – This is when the receiving team scores a point. In the old days, you had to serve to score, and this was called side-out scoring. Now, we have rally scoring, and points are scored regardless of which side serves.
- **Transition** – Normally, this refers to the move from defense to offense, but it can also describe any change from one system to another. (Serve to defense, offense to coverage, coverage to defense, etc.)
- Offense is often divided into different categories:
    - **Serve-receive offense** – Offense after the opponent's serve.
    - **Transition offense** – Offense after defending an opponent's attack.
    - **In-system offense** – This is when there is an accurate pass to a setter, who then has every setting option.
    - **Out-of-system offense** – This is when an inaccurate pass either severely limits the setter's options

or is so bad that another player has to set it. Needless to say, every team is more effective scoring in-system.

Those should get you started. Your next challenge is to learn the rules.

TIP 6: KNOW THE RULES

The object of volleyball is quite simple – make the ball hit the floor on your opponent's side of the court while keeping it off the floor on your side. Though the object is straightforward, there are rules that aren't so clear, and you should know them. Here are seven of the most common, ranked in order of importance. I have also added some pithy commentary that may come in handy.

1. **Number of contacts**: In the indoor game, each side has up to three contacts, though it's four contacts if the ball hits the block. Many coaches are hung up on always using three contacts, believing that anything less is sacrilegious. If your team knocks the serve back over the net and scores a point, these coaches will treat you like a leper. I'm probably in the minority, but I say, "Good on ya!" Your team was able to get the ball to land on the opponent's side, and isn't that the object? Of course, as players become more skillful, this tactic will not be successful. I'm not advocating always passing it over on one, but if we're keeping score (and maybe we shouldn't be with beginners …) I'd rather win as an opportunist than lose as a purist. More important, my players would, too.

2. **Court boundaries:** Each side of the court is a 30 x 30 box, with an additional line running sideline to sideline 10 feet from the net (the 10-foot line). The sidelines and end-line are part of the court, so if a ball hits any part of a line, it's in. Similarly, 11 players need to be inside the "box" (not touching a line) when the ball is served, while the server must be outside the box. The server cannot touch the line, or it's a foot-fault and a loss of point. Once the ball is in play, players can move outside the boundaries. Two antennas (candy canes) are attached to the net above the sidelines; legal attacks must travel inside these without touching them. Finally, it's a violation to touch the net or to completely cross the center-line under the net. The under-the-net rule is a good one since it's dangerous to cross under the net when players are jumping. Sprained and broken ankles often result, so it's important to keep your players' feet on your side of the court.

3. **Rotation and substitutes:** Players begin in one of the six spots on the court and rotate clockwise after each side-out. Players must remain in the same serving order throughout each set. Serving out of order will cost you a point. Though different volleyball organizations allow different numbers of substitutes, once a sub enters a game in a certain spot in the rotation, she must remain in that same place. Likewise, if the original starter re-enters the game, she must replace the player who subbed for her. This rule prevents a team from subbing out its best attacker when she rotates to the back row and immediately inserting her back into left front. The rotation and sub rules have some important coaching implications. Take it from a guy who has learned the hard way; making sub/server mistakes is

embarrassing. Get a pencil and paper and keep track of your subs and your serving order as well!

4. **Overlap:** When the ball is served, players must be in rotational order. This is defined in relation to adjacent players rather than position on the court. That is, all six players could stand in the RB corner, as long as they maintained their positions in the rotation relative to players adjacent to them. As an example, MF has to be in front of MB and between LF and RF.

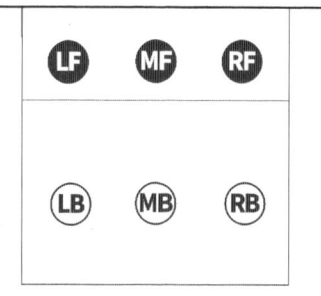

Rotational order

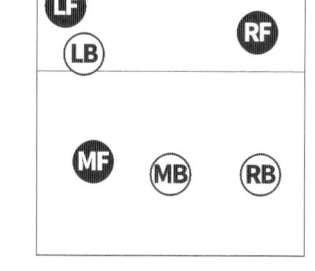

Example serve receive formation

If MB is in front of MF when the ball is served, this is an "overlap" violation and results in a loss of point. Because the server is outside the court boundaries, she is the only player who isn't bound by overlap rules.

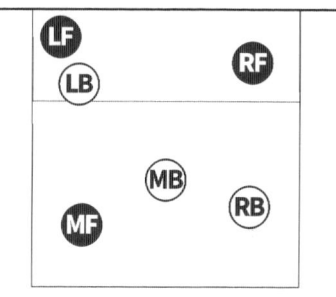

Example overlap violation

5. **Back row attack:** Players in the back row cannot attack a ball if they are in front of the 10-foot line and the ball is above the plane of the net. This is a back row attack violation and results in a loss of point. This violation commonly occurs when a back row setter tries to handle a pass that is close to the net and hits it over. This is one reason I don't recommend using back row setting systems for inexperienced teams.

6. **The libero:** Many casual volleyball observers ask me, "What's up with the little person in the colored jersey? Is that a fashion statement?" Nope, it's the libero. The libero is a dedicated back row player and a "free" sub who doesn't count against your sub limit. This explains the latin root origin (lib as in liberty and liberation). The libero is generally one of the best serve-receivers and best defenders on the team. To prevent coaches from expanding their role, the rules prohibit liberos from attacking any ball above the plane of the net (both front row and back row) or hand-setting in front of the 10-foot line. In addition to their defensive responsibilities, more and more teams are designating their liberos as secondary setters. That is, when the setter digs, the libero will set.

7. **Double contact:** I saved this one for last because every time I think about it, I get angry. In general, players can "double" a ball on first contact but not on the second or third contact. I know, it's stupid and makes no sense, but it gets worse. Referees of youth volleyball are often more stringent with their requirements for a legal set than referees of professional volleyball. See, now you're angry too.

Those are the most important rules. Of course, there are others, but we'll leave those to the refs. We have some coaching work to do.

PART 2:
HOW DO I START MY TEAM?

TIP 7: DETERMINE YOUR TEAM'S LEVEL

Before jumping into coaching, it's important that you know the level of your team. If coaches aren't in tune with their team's level, establishing the appropriate training priorities is impossible. Nothing damages a coach's credibility like a mismatch of level and training.

I made this mistake when I became a college men's assistant coach early in my career. I spent a bunch of time teaching serve-receive footwork patterns that worked so well for my high school girls' team. Unfortunately, this had little impact on the men's program; we needed to hit and block better to compete with the teams we played. Looking back, it's hardly surprising that I struggled to gain the respect of the players.

A more common mismatch is when a coach expects to be teaching teams how to pass-set-attack but the level is so low that only serving and ace prevention affects the outcome. This coach spends a lot of practice time tossing balls to a setter, who sets a line of attackers. Lo and behold, the match starts and the team is aced on seven out of every 10 serves. When it isn't an ace, the passes are nowhere near the setter and pandemonium ensues. For this reason, I placed "Determine Your Team's Level" as my first tip for this section, even before the tryout suggestions.

So how do you quickly determine the level? A coaching buddy of mine, Kyle Mashima (founder of the stat programs Rotate 123 and SoloStats), has developed a simple, effective method built on serving and ace prevention. I call it ace prevention rather than passing because it's really not about passing to the setter at the low levels; it's about not getting aced. Here is the statistical breakdown:

- **Beginning team:** Over 50% of serves to this team result in aces.
- **Beginning/Intermediate:** Aced between 30-50% of the time.
- **Intermediate/Advanced:** Aced 15-30% of the time.
- **Advanced:** Aced under 15% of the time.

This single stat makes the importance of ace prevention abundantly clear, for beginners and intermediate players alike. Of course, I don't expect you to complete an in-depth stats analysis before making your determination. However, these simple guidelines should get you started. If it quickly becomes apparent that your players don't have the depth perception to get behind a served ball (or even a thrown ball at the beginning), you know that you have a **Beginning** or

Beginning/Intermediate group. If your players are comfortable judging the depth of a served ball and controlling it to the setter, you can then begin to prioritize some skills other than serving and ace prevention.

We'll get into specifics for each level in Tip #25.

TIP 8: TRYOUTS, PART I – ALIGN YOUR TEAM SIZE WITH YOUR GOALS

When you enter the gym on day one, it's rare that the team has already been assembled. Often there will be a tryout phase; this might be a one-day evaluation, or it could be multiple days. The most difficult situations involve a large number of players (50 or more) trying out for spots on a single team (10-16 players). Cutting kids is brutal, so it's far more common for this large group to be divided into several different teams, usually by ability level. Tryouts will still be a good tool for evaluation, but rather than getting cut and walking out of the gym, players who are less experienced and less skilled are simply assigned to a lower level team.

I'm a big fan of giving everyone a chance to play, and I believe there are creative ways to avoid cutting kids. These include:

- Playing outside rather than in a gym.
- Running intramurals rather than focusing on outside competition.
- Establishing practice squads whose members might only practice and not compete.

Though these might not be equal to the most desirable situations (in the gym with fancy uniforms), they do give kids who love volleyball a chance to be part of a team. For me, that outweighs all of the pragmatic reasons to cut a young player.

What is the ideal team size? There's no simple answer; it depends on your situation. Most volleyball teams have between 10-14 players. Keeping a greater number of players allows you to play more 6v6 in practice, even if a couple of players are injured. It also gives you more depth. Fewer players on a team can be even more advantageous. Each player will get more reps in practice, and a smaller team makes it far easier to define clear playing roles and give everyone adequate playing time in matches. Of course, this generally results in happy players and even happier parents.

Before making your decision on team size, you should come to terms with your own take on winning/losing as well as the philosophy of your institution when it comes to playing time. Balancing winning with player development will be among your greatest challenges. Will you play a weaker lineup and lose for the sake of development? Or will you go for the win and leave your weaker players on the bench? Whatever you decide, your team size should be aligned with your philosophy; the larger the team, the more difficult it is to balance winning with development.

I ran a developmental club for many years that fielded only 12-under and 14-under girls' teams. Whenever possible, we limited the team to 9-10 players. That way, subbing was relatively easy in matches that went insanely fast (lots of aces). I could play everyone but still keep our most talented players on the floor in all ultra-competitive games. Of course, my situation was unusual because my gym fees were below average, so I didn't need large teams to make the revenue numbers work. Also, since we trained our teams together in large groups, I never had an issue with lack of 6v6 play in practice. The small teams were wonderful, but my setup was far from the norm.

My high school varsity team is much different. I usually keep 14 players. We had 16 one year, but that was cumbersome. We are a competitive program, and since winning is important to us, there might be 10 players who play a lot and four others who play very little. We've had good luck keeping these players positively engaged, but it takes a lot of work. It starts in the tryout phase when players often know if they are on the "bubble." I'm brutally honest with them, and if I decide there's a spot for them on the team, I will not let them have it until they go home, talk to their family about the role that I've outlined, and then commit to not just accepting that role but embracing it. Once a player agrees, I do everything I can to value her unique contribution to the team.

In addition to varsity, we field JV and FS (Frosh-Soph) teams. These vary in size, depending on the year. Our school is small enough that we never have to cut a freshman or sophomore. However, that often makes the junior season a difficult one, especially if we have a big group of talented younger players.

Since our school runs 6th-12th grade, we also offer middle school volleyball. Last season we had 54 players on four teams, with the fourth being an 18-player intramural group mostly comprised of 6th graders playing for the first time. Our three other teams had 12 players each, and they competed against other schools.

Just remember, if you begin with 60 players, 16 might seem like a small number. However, you have to think of that 16 as 6 players on the court and 10 others staring at you – along with their 20 parents.

TIP 9: TRYOUTS, PART II – MAKE YOUR FIRST IMPRESSION A GREAT ONE

Players will nervously enter the tryout gym, determined to make a good first impression. Coaches must remember they are also making a first impression, and they only have one chance. If there are difficult cuts to make, everything they do may be scrutinized by a disgruntled player, irate parent or pressured administrator. Here are some handy suggestions to help you get a great start:

1. **Organize beforehand:** To save time, bring a typed list of players who are trying out. Plan ahead so most of your time is spent evaluating rather than doing administrative tasks. Be sure you can easily identify players, whether it be by nametags or big numbers pinned on their shirts. Players sit in classrooms all day, and they have a good nose for teacher planning. Be prepared! Your credibility is on the line.

2. **Physical testing:** Some coaches don't want to spend the time, but I do this first. I want the best athletes to be recognized as the best athletes. That way, they may stick with volleyball instead of finding another sport to display their athleticism. Two quick tests are the standing broad jump (lower body explosiveness) and the two-hand basketball

chest pass for distance (upper body strength). Vertical jump is another that is often used, but whatever you choose, do it quickly. You want to spend the majority of the time observing volleyball skills.

3. **Evaluation form:** If you have a large group of players and a number of coaches evaluating, creating a standard form will help. Simple is best. Ranking the six skills (serving, serve-receive passing, setting, attacking, blocking, and digging) using a 4-1 grade scale is one way, with 4 as an "A" and 1 as a "D." Use the same ranking for the physical testing. It's important to note that this form is only a tool. Be careful. A player might rank as a 4 in serving and a 1 for everything else, and if you're coaching beginners, she could be your MVP.

4. **Intangibles:** You should also add a couple of categories for intangibles. One of the challenging aspects of tryouts is predicting the future. Two players might be the same today, but what about in eight weeks when you play your most important matches? For me, useful additions include: Motor (does the player naturally go for every ball?), Learning (does the player listen, process and attempt to implement feedback?) and Adversity (after a mistake, is the player more scared or resolved?). There is no magic to my list, so feel free to select your own categories that reflect your priorities. Whatever you decide, players who score well in the intangibles often possess a far higher ceiling than those who don't.

5. **Eyes on the prize:** Many coaches make errors in tryouts because it's so easy to get distracted. The best players

are often the biggest distraction; your eyes are naturally drawn to skillful athletes. The least experienced can also be distracting. However, the difficult decisions invariably involve the group in the middle. The faster you can isolate them, the better. In my varsity tryout, I might invite between 20-22 players for the team of 14. After two days, I will make a first cut (those usually become top JV players), and then I will have 16-17 remaining. At that point, I'll pull out the top players and let those battling for a spot have center stage. That way, my eyes (and my assistants') are focused on the task at hand. Finally, I always solicit my assistants' opinions separately before I tell them mine. I don't want bias to interfere.

6. **Communicating the results:** Doing this in an empathetic, respectful way can be a challenge. On my varsity, the final cuts are usually difficult ones, and I'll always meet with the players individually. Let's say I have four players for two spots; I'll put the rest of the players in some end of practice competition, and then conduct a short, private meeting with each player. After the meeting, those four will leave the gym. That way, they can choose to share or not share the results in their own way. In large group tryouts, individual meetings may be too cumbersome, but communicating the results in the most empathetic way possible is still necessary.

As far as a specific plan for tryouts, the general plan will resemble a well-crafted practice. We'll get into that in Part 4.

TIP 10: ESTABLISH STANDARDS OF BEHAVIOR

Early in my coaching career, I distributed a list of rules to players and painstakingly reviewed them to convince myself that there was complete clarity. Invariably, players would commit some infraction that didn't fit neatly into my list of rules, so the list grew. Eventually, I abandoned the rules, and instead created two constructs: a list of expectations and a small number of standards that are directly connected to our program's values.

Expectations: At our parent meeting (more on that in Tip #11), I distribute an expectation sheet that is divided into three sections outlining specific expectations for Players, Coaches and Parents. Given this format, it is clear that for our program to be successful, all of the stakeholders have responsibilities. Because I include a list of what players and parents can expect from coaches, I am accountable as well. If I expect the players to be on time, then I should be on time. Furthermore, I should respect the players' time by ending practices at the published time, not keeping them for lengthy meetings after matches.

This expectation sheet is a simple, one-page document with eight expectations for coaches and seven each for players and parents. In addition to basic attendance issues, I also tackle other big-ticket items like communication, sportsmanship, selflessness and responsibility.

ETA standards: I share the Expectation Sheet with both players and parents, but our ETA standards, which stand for Effort, Teamness and Attitude, are only for the players. I want these to be part of each player's (and coach's) commitment to the team. We have six standards, two for each of our values.

Effort
- We habitually give our best effort – mental, physical and emotional.
- We are great learners.

Teamness
- We take pride in forging strong relationships with all of our teammates.
- We relish opportunities to sacrifice for the good of the team.

Attitude
- Our contagious, positive attitudes set us apart.
- Our positive mindset is most apparent when we face adversity.

Unlike my old list of rules that became more complex over time, our current expectations and standards are simple and clear. We also state them in the positive – not what we shouldn't do but what we do. The evolution of my team rules has also changed my leadership style. Rather than "catching" players breaking rules and doling out punishment, I now commit to work with players whose behaviors aren't aligned with our values in order to teach life lessons. Of course, teaching these lessons is no less challenging and frustrating than it was 30 years ago, but our proactive approach characterized by the daily reinforcement of our values and our culture has worked for us. Over the years, we've had fewer and fewer misalignment issues.

So, here is a quick recap:

1. Keep the rules simple and general.
2. Connect them to your values and culture.
3. Be proactive; reinforce your values and culture on a daily basis.
4. Immediately address misaligned behaviors. The longer you wait, the more they will negatively impact your program.

TIP 11: HONE YOUR COMMUNICATION SKILLS (PART I) – EMPLOY THE RULES OF 3, 10 AND 30

If we were to create a list of qualities that all great coaches share, clarity in communication would rank high on the list. Here are a few communication techniques that have worked for me over the years:

The Rule of Three – I would love to claim ownership of this, but I just adopted it after hearing the concept on *The Basketball Podcast with Chris Oliver.* The Rule of Three states that we should communicate in chunks of three points or fewer. Examples include our values: Effort, Teamness and Attitude, as well as this three-pronged rules concept we are now exploring. This is a handy tool when it comes to player retention because communication is not what we say, it's what players comprehend.

Here is a more specific teaching example, a three-step prep for serve-receive. The first step is to *Identify Position.* That is, the player must make sure that she is in rotation and positioned correctly in relation to the sideline, the end-line and her teammates. Secondly, she must *Communicate Seam Responsibilities.* These might change depending on the position of the server, so they need to be confirmed before each serve. Finally, the passer must put her *Eyes on the Server.* It's critical that every passer is on the lookout for all the clues that the server will provide regarding the serve's speed, spin and location. Now I have an effective little acronym, ICE, and it's a great example of **The Rule of Three.** It not only reminds our players of their three responsibilities, it also reinforces the idea that we will be cool under pressure.

The Rule of 10 – This states that practice activities should be no longer than 10 minutes. Though this isn't strictly a communication rule, it nevertheless frames our communication and reminds us to teach in small chunks. As a young coach, I had no clue, and I'd often keep teams in drills "until they got it right." I'd be piling on feedback, and the situation would often move from bad to worse. As a savvy old guy, I now understand that 30 minutes of serving is much less effective in a single time block. It's far better to distribute the serving into six blocks of five minutes.

The Rule of 30 – This one limits any coaching explanation to 30 seconds. This can be challenging for many coaches, but it's vital that we strive for both brevity and clarity. After 30 seconds, we hit a point of diminishing returns and players' attention will lag. Even if every detail isn't crystal clear, put them back on the court. Your players will not only learn more, they will be playing more, standing less, and having more fun.

These rules are recent additions to my coaching toolbox, and they've helped me sharpen my communication skills. Give them a try!

TIP 12: HONE YOUR COMMUNICATION SKILLS (PART II) – PRAISE IN PUBLIC AND CORRECT IN PUBLIC

This might seem a bit harsh, but let me explain. My first challenge as a coach is to teach our players the difference between "correcting" and "criticizing." Players often believe these terms are synonymous, but they need to understand that for us to be our best, I have to error-correct often and criticize rarely. To teach them the importance of error-correction, we begin with the four stages of learning:

- **Unconscious incompetence:** You don't know what you don't know.
- **Conscious incompetence:** You know what the error is now.
- **Conscious competence:** You have corrected the error, but you have to think about it.
- **Unconscious competence:** You perform the skill correctly and without any conscious thought.

I'll take them through a quick example using the attack approach. In PE class, if you set a freshman football player, he'll usually take a running broad jump off one foot and fly into the net. This is *Unconscious Incompetence*. Of course, to protect themselves from injury, the opponents' blockers will tell him, "Hey, quit jumping into the net; you're going to hurt somebody!" Now he's moved to *Conscious Incompetence*. He still has this wild technique, but he knows that there's a better way. He then asks a volleyball player to teach him the steps, and as he begins to practice ("Left-right-left), he's in the third stage, *Conscious Competence*. He is performing the approach correctly, but he has to think about his feet. Finally, three years later, he's abandoned football, and he's the star OH on the volleyball team. He takes hundreds of approaches each week, and he never thinks about the footwork. He's now *Unconsciously Competent*.

Once our players understand this, they see the importance of my role in helping them move from Stage 1 to Stage 2. As an example, let's say that a MB never moves off the net to prepare to attack after blocking. Instead, she stays at the net. If I don't point this out, she will never improve. She'll be stuck in Stage 1. Furthermore, if I correct her in private, I am losing the opportunity to teach five of her teammates who also rarely transition after blocking. That's why it's important for me to correct in public; there are other players who deserve to be coached. I shouldn't deny them the opportunity to learn as fast as possible because I'm worried that a simple error-correction is going to have lasting damage on a player's self-esteem.

With that said, it's critical that I preserve the player's dignity when I error-correct, and some players need more TLC than others. There are countless ways to do this, but a simple one is to immediately create controlled situations, so I can catch the player doing it right. I might say, "Julie now understands transitioning, so we are going to set her three balls." In order to attack, she has to transition. Each time she does it, I celebrate like crazy! What began as an error-correction ends as a celebration.

TIP 13: HONE YOUR COMMUNICATION SKILLS (PART III) – USE GUIDED DISCOVERY

John Kessel recently retired from a long career as a master coaching guru at USA Volleyball, and he's had a profound influence on my coaching. His biggest impact was teaching me about **Guided Discovery**. Let's start with this quote from French poet Antoine de Saint-Exupéry: "If you want to build a ship, don't drum up people together to collect the wood, and don't assign them tasks and work. But rather teach them to long for the endless immensity of the sea." This provides a perfect starting point for *Guided Discovery*. It begins with inspiration, a vision of joyful, exhilarating play that pulls players toward the goal rather than a task-master paradigm that pushes them.

From there, we can use techniques like the Socratic method to help us. A simple definition is "asking" more and "telling" less. Now, there are many times when "telling" is the simplest and quickest way to communicate. However, if I want to stimulate deep learning, using curiosity is an effective tool. Since I coach at a prep school that values academics, I can easily leverage our players' intellect by asking pointed questions to challenge them. Surprisingly, though they are challenged on a daily basis in the classroom, they are often uncomfortable with this in the gym. They are so accustomed to being "told," their default is, "Just tell me what to do." It's my responsibility to move them out of this comfort zone.

For our young players, I start simple by using questions with two choices. "In serve-receive, do you think it's better to have more weight on one foot or weight evenly distributed on both feet? Why?" The "why" is always a part of the questioning process. The more they understand why, the "stickier" the learning. As players gain experience, the questions become more complex. For instance, "What is the fastest way for you to transition? Why?" or "How should we attack their rotation defense?" The fun part of *Guided Discovery* for me is when our players begin to ask challenging questions; that's when I know that they are truly engaged in the learning process.

Another recent focus for me is diction, or word choice. I have become much more aware of my vocabulary that is not aligned with *Guided Discovery*. I am working to eliminate phrases like, "You gotta," as in, "You gotta transition!" or "You gotta cover!" Instead, I am using words like "challenge," as in, "The 'challenge' for you is to cover your hitter." I can then follow up with a question. "What are some strategies we can employ to help remind everyone to cover?" A couple of other new phrases for me include: "Let's experiment with…." or "Take me through your thought process."

Slowly but surely, this old dog is learning some new tricks by using *Guided Discovery* techniques to help players take more responsibility on their respective paths to improvement. Instead of me shoving them down a path, they now are blazing their own trails and using me to help problem-solve along the way.

TIP 14: COACH PARENTS, TOO

When I began coaching back in the 1980s, the majority of volleyball parents were simply happy to see their kids involved in a sport. Oh, how the times have changed!

We are all responsible for creating a crazy youth sports culture where parents are compelled to make huge investments of time and money so their kids can compete in their sport of choice. Furthermore, because the level of play is so much higher than it was in the past, parents are more likely to become fans – fanatics! It's not surprising that they often become over-involved.

In this new paradigm, coaching the parents is an important part of my job. If I neglect it, I run the risk of the parents being led by the most "knowledgeable" one in the group. Let me explain the problem here. This "knowledgeable" parent probably had some experience in the sport or had an older child who played. If this parent happens to be the over-involved type, the type that second-guesses every coaching decision, then I suddenly have a major problem. It's not merely one rogue parent; it's a leader who is providing free rogue parent training!

So, I must train the parents before someone else does. The goal is to create a group of **great sports parents**. Here are my teaching points:

1. Parents can either be an asset or a hindrance to the team. We expect every parent to be an asset. The goal is to be a great sports parent.

2. Great sports parents know that their primary role is to support the players and coaches who are testing themselves in the public arena.
3. Great sports parents help coaches teach selflessness over selfishness. Being a great teammate involves sacrifice for the good of the group, and great sports parents help us to reinforce this critical lesson.
4. Great sports parents might second-guess coaches in private, but they NEVER do it in front of other parents or in front of their daughters. If they do, they are sowing the seeds of discontent and working *against* the team rather than for it.
5. Great sports parents are more concerned with players learning life lessons than winning any particular match. They are parents before they are fans, and they understand the learning opportunities that losing provides.

I adopted a concept from the Positive Coaching Alliance to reinforce these parent behaviors. It's called the *Culture Keeper*. In my high school program, this is the primary responsibility of our team parents. In the old days, providing orange slices was their top priority; now, ensuring that our parents are striving for greatness is priority one.

Of course, I can't ask these parents to be great if they don't see me striving for greatness. That's why it's imperative for me to be a responsible professional. First, I have to be empathetic and understand how difficult it is to be a great sports parent. In the current youth sports culture, this isn't easy. Secondly, I have to communicate consistently, both with "little stuff" like scheduling and transportation and "big stuff" like playing time philosophy and role definition. If I'm doing my best in these areas, I can ask them to be their best as well.

By and large, I'm grateful for the supportive parents we've had over the years. However, I can take nothing for granted. I don't stop coaching our team after we play well, and I can't stop coaching the parents either. There are powerful forces pulling them away from being great sports parents, so I must remain vigilant in my training. It takes some work, but it's well worth it. Nothing is more fun than when everyone in the program is rowing in the same direction!

TIP 15: USE CAPTAINS TO REINFORCE YOUR CULTURE

Though some coaches are skeptical of the concept of team captains, I'm a believer. Captains can reinforce our culture in ways that I cannot. If you decide to have captains on your team, it's important to take time to train them. Before that can occur, there is always the dicey issue of selection.

Here's how it works in my high school program. At the end of every season, we meet as a team, and in addition to turning in their uniforms and completing a coaching evaluation, all players vote for the following season's captains. I take some time to prep our players before the vote. The captains in our program shoulder considerable responsibility, and I make it very clear that each player's vote is the first important act for the new season.

The unusual part of this tradition is that we include our graduating seniors in the process, even though they won't be on the team. For us, it makes perfect sense. Part of the seniors' legacy includes their votes for our future leaders. These seniors have seen the underclassmen at their best and at their worst. That is precisely why we value the seniors' votes, and why we do not solicit votes from new varsity players. New players who join in the fall do not have enough information to vote wisely. They haven't been part of our culture, and they haven't yet been through the ups and downs of a competitive season.

We usually settle on the two players receiving the most votes, and we announce the captains at our end-of-season banquet. That announcement ends one season and begins another. I now have the off-season to engage in leadership training. We've had good luck using Jeff Janssen's book, *The Team Captain's Leadership Manual*. We'll complete two chapters per month, and I'll ask our captains to send me their reading notes. Our new captains also get some practical training since they lead our voluntary off-season strength workouts.

By the time our season begins, I have a good working relationship with the captains. They are ready to execute their primary responsibilities, which include:

- Modeling our values (ETA)
- Keeping everyone connected
- Communicating with me

I often use the captains as a sounding board, and I can't tell you how many times they've prevented me from doing something stupid. I'll even use them mid-match when I'm deciding on a timeout. If an opponent scores a couple of unanswered points, I might give the captain a look and say, "Now?" She'll either nod or say, "One more." It's fun when she keeps us out there, and we respond with a point. She'll then give me that, "I told you so" look, the one that I see so often from my wife.

Our tradition of captain selection has worked well for us, but it's not for everyone. Some coaches believe that any player vote becomes a popularity contest, so they always choose the captains. Other coaches split the difference; they choose one, and the players choose one. I like to put it in the context of life lessons. These players will soon be voting for their political leaders; if society can trust them for that, then surely I can trust them to wisely choose team leaders.

Though I'm a big proponent of captains for my high school program, I don't designate captains for my 12- and 14-under club teams. Everyone takes a turn at the pre-game coin toss, and our leadership training is much more generic. For me, captains have been a great benefit to our high school program with its four-year window of development. Club is a different beast, and I've chosen an alternative leadership route with those young players.

Whatever you decide, just remember this: Selection is only the beginning. If you want your leaders to lead, you must allot some time to teach them how to do it.

PART 3:
HOW DO I TEACH THE SKILLS?

TIP 16: USE KEY WORDS TO CHUNK INFORMATION

This is a lesson I learned early in my coaching career, and if I remember correctly, my source was Brian Gimmillaro, who won three NCAA championships as head coach of the Long Beach State women's team. He was a master teacher when it came to volleyball skills, and one of his secrets was the use of keywords. For each skill, he would have a small number of keywords (3-5), and each word would represent a considerable amount of information. This allows for faster teaching and learning since coaches are using a single word to substitute for a large chunk of feedback.

For example, our first key for passing is Posture. This single word includes the following information:

- Feet are nearly parallel, with the right foot leading slightly.
- Weight is evenly distributed on the balls of both feet.
- Knees are flexed athletically.
- Player is slightly leaning forward with knees in front of toes and shoulders in front of knees.
- Arms are straight, relaxed and hanging.

In the beginning, I just adopted all of Brian's keys, but over the years, my keywords evolved and became my own. I'm always on the lookout for words that will provide the simplest and clearest description possible. One example of a recent change in my serving keys is the substitution of *Hammer* for *Punch*.

With *Punch*, we had too many players who interpreted this as a "shot-put" motion; *Hammer* more accurately describes the elbow's job (leading the wrist, rather than following it) in the serve, and it has worked much better for us.

In addition to the use of keywords, there are two concepts that connect all of our skills instruction. They are balance and efficiency. In every volleyball skill, the better the player's balance, the more consistent the skill's execution. This becomes quite obvious when beginners and experts play side by side. The experts make it look so easy, while the beginners are falling all over the place.

For efficiency, we want the movements as simple as possible, with no wasted motion. Think of a 10-year-old shooting a 3-pointer in basketball, and then think of Steph Curry. Steph's simple, efficient motion is easy to repeat, and that's a big reason he is one of the most accurate shooters in NBA history. We want the same for our players. Simple, efficient movements will result in more consistent serves, passes, sets and attacks.

TIP 17: START WITH MOVEMENT

This may seem a bit counterintuitive, given that mastering volleyball involves learning a number of specific skills that are not as easily accessible as skills in other sports. For instance, everybody throws a ball before playing baseball or softball, but very few people pass a ball with their forearms or set a ball before they play volleyball. Nevertheless, I'm a believer in starting volleyball instruction with movement, though I quickly move on to volleyball skills and games. Here is why starting with movement makes sense:

Getting players into movement at the outset challenges them athletically. The first movement skill I teach is sprinting, simply pursuing a ball and preventing it from hitting the ground. This challenges our best athletes, and it demonstrates to them that volleyball is a game that will reward their athleticism. If I were to begin with static passing, the best athletes might not be much better than the worst. When it comes to rebounding a ball off their forearms, the difference could be negligible. In that situation, those top athletes might decide that volleyball isn't the sport for them, and they might not show up on day two.

Here is a short list of the specific movements we teach in the order we present them:

1. **Sprinting and pursuit:** We begin with having players pursue a ball and catch it. They need to do everything possible to keep the ball off the floor. It's fun to see aggressive athletes flying around the gym and even hitting the floor. They might not know a thing about volleyball, but how cool is it to see them diving on the floor in the first 5 minutes of a day one practice!

   We teach sprinting and pursuit before we teach any volleyball skills. The following movement skills come later and are integrated into the volleyball training. We can also isolate them in our practice warmup. Why jog in warmups when you can do specific, game-related footwork patterns?

2. **Step-shuffle footwork:** This is simple 3-step serve-receive footwork. Players begin in *posture* with feet at shoulder width. They step in a direction, then shuffle (move both feet) to rebalance and end in the exact same posture. Players need to be comfortable step-shuffling in any direction.

3. **Attacking approach:** There is a bit of disagreement in some coaching circles regarding the advantages of a 3-step or 4-step approach. I begin teaching a 2-step approach and then add steps so players learn 2-, 3-, and 4-step approaches. For right-handers, the 4-step sequence is Right, Left, Right-Left. The approach steps should be small to big and slow to fast.

4. **Open up:** We teach beginners to move behind the ball to play it. If a front row player can't get her core behind the

ball, she should "open up" so a back row player can make the play. This open up move is a pivot and double-shuffle.

5. **Backing up:** Whenever possible, we back up the defender who is the player contacting the ball. This prevents balls from landing if a player "bails out," and it also puts us in position to pursue if a ball is shanked backwards.

These are the first five movements we teach, and then later on we add the **drop step-shuffle** (for deep balls in serve-receive that we lateral pass), **attacker transition** (the opposite of an approach, these are the steps off the net to prepare to attack) and **blocking** (we begin with the same step-shuffle we use for passing).

Communication: For each of the footwork patterns, there is accompanying communication, so we always combine the training. Examples include **step-shuffle** – call "Mine"; **attack approach** – call the type of set you want; **open up** – call "Deep."

TIP 18: INTEGRATE READING INTO EVERY SKILL YOU TEACH

I've mentioned the wisdom of John Kessel in a couple of prior tips, and I have to credit him here as well. John's favorite clinic question is, "What is the premier skill in volleyball?" Coaches will shout out the traditional answers of serving or passing, but John will then give the answer and immediately launch into the gospel of "reading."

Reading is simply picking up cues that help predict future events. Reading is involved in all volleyball skills, and players who learn to read at a young age progress at a much faster rate than ones who don't. Teaching reading is counterintuitive; players in all sports are often admonished to "keep your eye on the ball." However, to read well, players must take their eyes off the ball. The ball will not tell you where it's going, but the player about to make contact with it will give you all kinds of useful information.

Most beginners think reading is only for defenders, but every skill in volleyball involves reading. Here is a short breakdown:

Defenders/blockers: They need to take their eyes off the ball and focus on the attacker. Attacker posture, relationship of shoulder to the ball, and speed of arm are all important indicators. The best defenders have a large database of situations and results, and they are always adding useful information. They then adjust their defense position accordingly.

Serve-receivers: Passers will read servers by observing their posture (facing which direction?), the placement of their toss and the speed of their arm. Server "history" – where did she serve before? – is also part of the passer's database.

Setters: They must be able to pick up cues from the passers and diggers that will help them get a good "jump" on the ball. Secondly, they need to be aware of the position of their attackers. If an attacker hits the floor to dig a ball, she's probably not ready for a fast-tempo set.

Attackers: They must be able to read the setter to help determine the set location. In addition, the best attackers can accurately predict the positioning of the opponents' blockers and defenders.

Servers: They should pick up cues from the opponents' serve-receivers that reveal weaknesses in the formation. Perhaps they are trying to "hide" a weak passer, or perhaps the placement of the serve can eliminate their favorite attacking route.

Using **Guided Discovery** (see Tip #13) is a perfect strategy for teaching reading. Common questions to employ include, "What did you see there?", "Did the attacker/server give you any tells?", or "What adjustment should you make based on what you saw?"

TIP 19: TEACH ATTACKING FIRST

I like to begin by teaching pursuit, but the first traditional volleyball skill I teach is spiking. The reasons are simple. First, hitting is fun! We want players to fall in love with the sport, and there's no quicker way than to let them jump up and smack the ball over the net. Secondly, it's another opportunity to capture the best athletes and make sure they come back for more.

Attacking involves two separate skills: the arm swing and the approach. Though not every coach would agree, I teach them separately. It makes sense to begin with the arm swing because players can immediately get the satisfaction of seeing a spike go over the net. Here are the keywords for the attacking arm swing:

- **Backswing:** Loose, straight arms swing back and then swing up to assist with the jump.
- **Sight 90:** The left (non-hitting) arm sights the ball, and the right arm is pulled back at 90 degrees.
- **Elbow lead:** In order to accelerate the hand, the elbow must lead the wrist. (Avoid the shot put).
- **Lift and whip:** The loose attacking arm will extend up and accelerate through contact.

I will start the players with "dummy" arm swings – that is, swings with no ball. They can do one every three seconds, so it's easy for them to spend a minute or two before adding balls. Then they can toss to themselves and hit over the net. If the players are young beginners, don't be afraid to lower the net.

Here's a short list of my favorite feedback when teaching the arm swing:

- **Hide your logo:** The attacking arm is pulled back, and the front of your shirt faces sideways, not forward.
- **Crack:** Make a cracking sound by contacting the ball in the middle of a big, firm hand.
- **Shape and spin:** Impart topspin on the ball, and see it clear the net in a rainbow arc.
- **Way up:** Contact the ball on the way up in your jump, not the way down.

Once players have learned the arm swing keys, done a few dummy swings, and hit a bunch of self-tossed balls, I quickly move them to the approach. Here are my simple keys for the four-step approach:

- **Lean:** Start 12 to 15 feet off the net, right foot slightly ahead, sprinter's lean.
- **Right .... left, right, left.**
- **Two feet:** Jump off two feet and land on two feet.

And here's my favorite feedback for the attacking approach:

- **Walk to run:** Steps should be small to big, slow to fast.
- **Left step:** The second (left step) should be behind or on the 10-foot line.
- **Quiet arms:** On the first two steps, arms are relaxed and hanging.

Once again, I don't wait for mastery; we advance to the whole skill as soon as possible. For beginners, we begin with a simple two-step approach, and then we toss (very low) for them to "tee-hit." We then progress to an antenna high toss that is delivered on the attacker's second step (left) of a four-step approach. We demand that players call their steps (Right … left, right, left), so the coach can toss at the proper time. It also helps attackers learn the slow-to-fast rhythm.

Teaching progressions is a bit out of fashion, but I'm still a believer. For all the progression-haters, I will concede that I spent far too long on each step in the past. Now, I'm more inclined to quickly move through the steps and get to the "whole" skill as soon as possible.

TIP 20: BECOME A TOPSPIN EXPERT

For me, wrist snap and topspin are two of the most misunderstood concepts in our sport. As an avid tennis player, I am a topspin freak, and if I had to choose my favorite tip, it's the one I'm going to talk about here.

First of all, words that you will never hear in our gym include "Hit over the ball," "Reach" and "Snap." I believe they do far more harm than good.

If I'm hitting a tennis ball, and I want to impart topspin, I move my racket from low to high on contact. The same principle applies to hitting a volleyball. To impart topspin, my hand needs to move from low to high on contact.

Let me debunk the traditional feedback terms mentioned above. If you imagine young hitters who cannot reach the top of the net, then you understand that hitting over the ball is not great feedback because this causes the ball's trajectory to go down, not up and over the net. Furthermore, if this young/short player is reaching at contact, odds are that her hand will be moving high to low at impact rather than low to high. Moving high to low is the perfect recipe for a hit into the bottom of the net. Finally, players who focus on snap are generally thinking of hitting the ball on a downward trajectory. That may be a wonderful technique for a 6-foot-8 Russian player, but it's not quite as effective for my 5-foot-3 seventh-grader.

So here are our substitutes:

- **Throw your hand *up* into the ball:** This will allow our attacker's hand to be moving low to high on contact. We want the orientation to go up, not down.

- **Bent elbow on contact:** We want our attackers to reach *after* contact, not *before*. The most common error for young attackers is that their arm is fully extended too early (no elbow bend), so the shoulder becomes the critical lever. In this situation, the only direction the hand can move is down. With a slightly bent elbow as the critical lever, the arm can extend up – low to high.

- **Palm up:** In any natural throwing motion, the wrist will naturally move forward or snap. It's not an action that needs attention. However, if we want young hitters to attack over the net, their palm needs to be facing up on contact, not down.

The other thing to remember here is what you celebrate. In my younger days, I celebrated the straight-down attack. This is an attack that would be blocked by most good teams, so my players were getting horrible feedback. Now, I celebrate the ball that is hit with heat (high velocity), clears the net with some space and lands in the deep corners.

I'll end with my biggest pet peeve – players warming up their arms by mindlessly hitting countless balls into the floor. This makes as much sense as warming up my serve in tennis by hitting balls into the ground. The game requires that the ball clear the net; let's practice that.

TIP 21: KNOW THE KEY TO TEACHING ATTACKER TIMING

This is something that I learned relatively late in my coaching career, and it's so simple that I'm a bit ashamed it took me so long to figure out. The critical timing variable for attackers is *the step they are taking when the ball is in the setter's hands.*

This elementary concept allows me to teach a fast offense, and it also provides a frame of reference for both our setters and our attackers. They can use this mechanism to communicate and be on the same page when it comes to timing.

Here are the general parameters:

- **Out-of-system high set** (set is 25-30 feet high, hand set or bump set): Attacker is not moving. She has not yet started her approach on setter contact.

- **Standard high tempo** (set is 15-20 feet high, often called a "4" or a "5"): On setter contact, the attacker is on the first right step of her 4-step approach.

- **Second tempo/"Go" set (to the left-side) or fast set to the right pin** (set is approximately antenna height – 10-12 feet): The attacker is on the second step of her approach on setter contact.

- **First tempo/Quick attack** (set is below antenna height, about 8-9 feet high): On setter contact, the attacker is getting ready to jump with her arms parallel to the ground.

- **Zero tempo** (low set is hit as it is coming out of the setter's hand): On setter contact, the attacker is already in the air.

By using video, we can give attackers very accurate feedback when it comes to "being on their steps." If we pause the video when the ball is in the setter's hands, we can observe the foot placement of each of our attackers.

Of course, there are some other variables involved, and the most important one is *space*. Let's say our OH is hitting a "Go" set on the left. We ask our setters to set the ball "antenna high" and, as mentioned above, our attacker would be on her second step (left) on setter contact. We can always rely on these timing parameters if the pass is perfect and the setter is in the target area.

However, what if the setter is two meters closer to the attacker? Or two meters farther away? If the ball is set at the same speed and height, then it will be up to the attacker to be:

- Farther into her approach when the ball is closer.
- More delayed when the ball is farther away.

Because of this, we added the terms "soft" and "hard" when talking about attackers' steps. That is, when the setter is farther away, the attacker might be on a "soft" left, just beginning to place her left foot on the floor. Conversely, if the setter is close to the attacker, the attacker would be on her "hard" left, coming off her left foot and ready for the final two steps.

This concept has helped me quickly teach my high school team to embrace a faster offense, especially with our sets to the pins. However, it's not limited to the more advanced teams. I can also use it as a teaching key for my middle school groups, emphasizing to young attackers how to stay behind the ball and approach slow to fast.

TIP 22: COMBINE PASSING AND SERVE-RECEIVE TRAINING

One of the best lessons I learned as a young coach was to base all passing instruction on the techniques needed for successful serve-receive. Whether it's a slow-moving free ball or a rocket serve, we use the same teaching keys and expect the same execution.

Let me explain why this is so important, especially for the beginning player. When players first start passing, it's natural for them to "walk into it." That is, the athlete will take a step forward and then use both the arms and legs to lift the ball. The majority of the player's weight is then placed on the lead leg. Beginners may find success passing back and forth using this method, but for serve-receive, it's a killer. Using this "free ball method" to pass in serve-receive is one reason many beginning teams are getting aced over 60% of the time.

Here are the three main problems:

1. If the athlete plays a serve with one foot in front and one in back, she doesn't have a stable base or lateral balance.

2. If the athlete is lifting with her legs, her torso and head move. We believe that keeping the head still (allowing players to keep their eyes still) makes it easier to contact the ball consistently on the "sweet spot" of the platform (approximately two inches above the wrist bone).

3. If a passer has all her weight on one foot, she can't move. This is why you'll often see beginners swing and completely miss a served ball.

On day one of passing instruction, the first key we teach is Posture. Players have their feet slightly wider than shoulder width with the right foot a bit in front of the left. **Their weight is evenly distributed on both feet.** From here, we teach step-shuffle movement, so players can move in any direction and still end up in this balanced "two-footed" posture. They begin with simple toss and catch in this posture, and we also expect them to keep arms straight and elbows locked throughout the process. This helps them simulate the spacing they need when they begin to pass.

At the beginning, the players will find this "two-footed" technique much more difficult than the "one-foot step-in" technique. We don't care! If we want players to be functional in serve-receive, they must have a stable base and be able to move. The quicker we can teach this, the better. If we let them use the comfortable technique for free balls, it will invariably delay their ability to become good at serve-receive.

For beginning teams, once the match begins, our focus on balance and movement often pays big dividends. If our passers can shuffle behind the ball and not get aced by the opponent's best server, we have addressed a critical variable and helped put our team in a much better position to win.

TIP 23: TEACH SERVE-RECEIVE PASSING WITH K-I-S-S

The Keep It Simple, Stupid mantra is a good one to remember when teaching the fundamental skill of passing. We've done this by making our teaching keys as basic as possible. They are all single words, so that helps make them "sticky" – that is, easy for our players to remember.

Here are our teaching keys for serve-receive passing:

- **Posture:** Stable base with feet just wider than shoulder width. Knees are flexed, and player's shoulders are in front of knees, and the knees are in front of feet. Arms are straight, relaxed and hanging.

- **Platform:** The wrists and forearms come together simultaneously. The thumbs are aligned and pushed down to lock the elbows. The platform is "long and strong."

- **One:** There is a single move of the platform to play the ball. There is no "bobbing" of the platform and no "wind-up."

- **Freeze:** Passers freeze their posture after contact. That allows them to check their balance and platform angle.

As I mentioned in the previous tip, we begin with a lot of catching, stressing the *4 B's* (**Butt Behind Ball, Balanced**). Though many coaches are teaching more lateral passing and are not as concerned with getting behind the ball, I'm more of a traditionalist. I believe in creating the simplest angle, and for beginners, the easiest angle is created with the passer's core behind the ball.

Here is some of my favorite feedback for passers:

- *Two feet* (stay balanced)
- *Face the ball, angle the platform*
- *Hands down*
- *Short stroke*

The last two need a bit more explanation. We differentiate beginning passers and advanced passers by the length and speed of their passing strokes. Beginners are often "lifters." That is, they begin with their platforms almost parallel to the floor and have a long, slow lifting motion. This makes it especially difficult to pass high velocity, low trajectory serves. The ball will often be shanked due to the relatively high platform angle. Advanced passers keep their hands down, and their passing stroke is short, quick and compact. This is a much more effective technique for controlling tough serves.

TIP 24: FOR SERVING, REMEMBER TO TEACH TEMPO

When we think of timing or tempo, we often think of attackers who mistakenly run in to attack before a ball is set.

However, coaches often overlook the impact of tempo when teaching the other skills in volleyball.

I believe that beginners in many sports often *prepare late but play the ball too early,* whereas experienced players *prepare early and play the ball late.* Once again, I am a tennis guy, so I like tennis analogies. The beginner in tennis doesn't prepare until after the incoming ball has already bounced and is almost on them. This novice then combines the prep and the swing into one wild motion, and the ball is often "pulled" to the left, meaning the swing is actually *too early.* Contrast this with Roger Federer; he prepares early and then pulls the trigger late and fast. He is a master of tempo.

For beginning servers, employing the serving keys is only half the battle; they also need to connect them with the proper tempo or timing. Beginners who have mastered throwing (like softball players) do this naturally. However, young players with underdeveloped throwing motions have to be taught the proper timing.

The secret is timing the server's step with the contact of the ball. Just after her foot hits the ground, the server should make contact with the ball. The longer the lag time between those two events, the greater the power loss for the server. This makes perfect sense, since the step is helping the server transfer power into the swing.

Here are my teaching keys for serving:

- **Ready:** Feet are at a 45-degree angle to the net. All the weight is on the back foot (right for right-handers, left for left-handers), and the feet are close together. The right arm is prepared with the elbow bent at 90 degrees, and the left arm is held out in front with the ball.

- **Lift:** This is a lift or "place" rather than a toss. The difference is that there is no "wind-up." The left hand merely lifts the ball about 24 inches high.

- **Step-hammer:** As mentioned above, these are interconnected. The server steps with her left foot, and then swings her arm, finishing with a hammer motion. Specifically, this means that the elbow leads the wrist.

Here are some of my favorite reminders:

- *Low lift*
- *Heel contact*
- *Tight wrist*
- *Make it float*
- *Swing fast / Faster*

Be careful about moving beginners back too quickly. They will be eager to get behind the end-line. My general rule of thumb is to always test them to see if they can throw the ball over the net from the end-line. If they can't do this, do not have them try to serve it from there because it will be a lesson in futility. Instead, start them at the 10-foot line. Each time the server gets three in a row in the court, she gets to take a giant step back.

My last tip for teaching beginners is to have them serve from the middle of the court. Beginners often toss the ball a bit behind them, so serves veer right (for right-handers). If they begin standing in the middle rather than the right side of the end-line, those serves will be in the court.

TIP 25: TEACH THE JUMP FLOAT, EARLY AND OFTEN

The jump float is the most effective serve in the women's game for a couple of reasons. First, the geometry is slightly better. The ball is contacted at a higher point and, since we teach the server to broad jump into the court, it is also contacted at a closer point. More important, the jump float is harder to read. The best serve-receivers have the best vision, but the jump float's added movements (approach and jump) help disguise the cues that passers use to determine the speed and location of the serve.

I recommend teaching the jump float serve as soon as possible, probably earlier than you might think is wise. Once servers become fairly consistent with the standing serve, have them experiment with the jump float. Though it's a bit more complex than the standing float, some young players will instantly be more effective when they add a short approach and jump.

Here are the simple teaching keys:

- **Ready:** Server stands in the same posture as the standing float, unless she chooses to toss with two hands instead of one. I prefer a one-handed toss, but if players are more comfortable and accurate with a two-handed toss, I don't change them.

- **Left – Lift:** Right-handers take a small, slow left step and then lift the ball in front of them.

- **Right-Left-Jump & Swing:** The right-left steps are bigger and faster than the first left step, and the player then broad jumps into the court and hits the serve.

Some players might prefer a 4-step approach; I don't think it makes much difference either way. Here is our most common feedback:

- *Lift in front*
- *Chase it*
- *Make it float*

As I mentioned at the outset, don't be afraid to experiment with this serve with young players. I used to wait until players had mastered a standing float before I introduced the jump float. That was a mistake. Now, I teach it far earlier in a player's development. Give it a go. You may be surprised at the results!

TIP 26: WHEN TEACHING SETTING, ASSIGN HOMEWORK

One of the current trends in coaching volleyball is more generalized training. Years ago, it was fashionable to focus on the unique skills of every position, so the training was more specialized. Setters worked on setting, middle blockers blocked, serve-receivers passed. Though this still holds true, the recent emphasis on out-of-system training has nudged many coaches to a more generalized approach. This is most evident when it comes to setting. At the high levels, coaches expect every player to set an accurate, high out-of-system ball. In addition, liberos are often trained as secondary setters, and they are now running the offense from behind the three-meter line.

For coaches of young, developing players, this is a great reminder that we should spend the time to teach every player the fundamentals of setting. However, for players to learn this unique skill, they need thousands of reps. If you use practice time for this, it will cut into your serving and ace-prevention training, and your team will suffer when competition begins. The simple remedy is to assign homework. Setting is the easiest skill for players to practice alone.

Let's start with the setting keys:

- **Left-Right:** This is the setting footwork, with the right toe pointed to the left-side target.

- **Shape:** The hands begin at waist level with the elbows bent at 90 degrees. The fingers are spread with the thumbs pointed at each other about 1-2 inches apart. The thumbs and index fingers form a triangle, with the index fingers also 1-2 inches apart.

- **Window:** With the hands already "shaped" and elbows remaining at 90 degrees, the shoulders generate the movement, putting the hands just above the forehead.

Players now look through the triangular window formed by their thumbs and index fingers.

- **Wrists:** The setting motion begins with the wrists flexing back, so the thumbs point back at the eyes. The ball is firmly stuck in the "wedge" of the thumbs and index fingers, though all the fingers touch the ball.

- **90-180:** The wrists then go forward, and the elbows follow, moving from their 90-degree position to locked out at 180 degrees.

- **Window:** On the follow-through, the elbows lock out, but the shape of the hands is constant. The triangle shape remains.

And here is some of my favorite feedback:

- *Point:* Aim the right toe toward the forward target.
- *Ball to hands* (not hands to ball): This is the tempo element. Rather than reaching up to attack the ball, let the ball come into the "wedge."
- *In the wedge:* The thumb and forefinger do more work than the other three fingers.
- *Thumbs to eyes:* The thumbs point back on contact, not down (lobster claws).
- *Flat finish:* Hands finish big and flat.

As you can see by the sheer number of words, the setting motion is the most nuanced of all the volleyball skills. In the beginning, we ask players to catch the ball on their window. It's important that they can both see and feel the ball in the triangular "wedge." Once players understand this concept, they can go home, lie on the bed, and begin to work on those thousands of necessary reps. From simple catching, they can progress to self-setting and wall setting.

The key is to give everyone this assignment, not just your setters.

TIP 27: TEACH PASSING AND PLATFORM (BUMP) SETTING AS TWO DISTINCT SKILLS

Normal people vacation in Paris, Hawaii or Cancun. Two summers ago, I made my way to Wichita, Kansas. The purpose was to spend some time with the coach of Wichita State, Chris Lamb. In addition to being one of the most successful coaches in college volleyball, Lambo might also be the most creative. He combines an insatiable curiosity with a fascination for numbers and meaningful statistics. He tops this off with a wildly competitive streak combined with an underdog's skepticism of the status quo. For me, this made Wichita the ideal vacation spot.

Of the many lessons I learned in the Wichita State gym, one of the most important was Coach Lamb's emphasis on out-of-system setting. He has coined his own term for the skill, "Tabletop," and it perfectly describes the critical differences between two platform skills: serve-receive passing and bump setting. While it might be tempting to combine the training of the two in the name of efficiency, that is a mistake. They require two distinct techniques.

For serve-receive, we ask players to use their shoulders to generate the force to pass. The passing "stroke" begins with the hands angled down to the ground so the platform's sweet spot is best exposed to the oncoming serve. Because we want to keep the head (eyes) as still as possible, we do not want players to lift their legs to generate force; the shoulders do the work.

The problem occurs when players use the serve-receive technique to bump set. The player starts her platform pointed down and then "swings" it upward in order to set the ball. During this swinging motion, the angle of the platform changes drastically, and if the timing isn't absolutely perfect, the accuracy of the set will suffer.

The tabletop move drastically improves the odds of an accurate set. In this technique, the platform begins parallel to the floor (hence, tabletop), and players use their legs to lift the set. Because the angle remains constant throughout the motion, timing isn't nearly as critical, and it's far easier to set more accurately and consistently.

This simple "tabletop" key has helped our bump setters become far more proficient in providing hittable out-of-system sets. Give it a try!

TIP 28: COMBINE FOREARM AND OVERHEAD DIGGING

One of the most under-trained skills in youth volleyball is overhead digging. Though I do not teach passers to use the overhead technique in serve-receive (I do think it's OK in emergencies), that is not a good reason to neglect it as a useful defensive technique.

I see young players consistently swing their platforms up behind their heads and consequently misplay balls that could easily be handled with an overhead dig. This is a coaching mistake, since we are not teaching this technique at the same time we teach platform digging. **For every ball a player digs with her platform, she should dig one overhead.**

My rationale is simple. If I spread my fingers and open my hands wide, I have a large surface area. In fact, it's probably 2-3 times as big as my platform's sweet spot. It makes no sense to use a platform with its relatively small surface compared with the overhead technique with its large one, especially if the ball is above your head!

Not only is overhead digging undertrained, I believe it is often mistrained as well. Many coaches teach their players to overlap or "cup" their hands. Their belief is that this creates a stronger surface, and balls cannot pass through their hands. This may be true, but the problem with this technique is the tiny surface area. To control the ball consistently is nearly impossible.

Instead, we should teach overhead digging with big, strong hands. They **look like setter's hands,** but there are critical differences between setting and overhead digging that many coaches neglect to teach. Here they are:

- Overhead diggers lock their wrists like blockers; setters' wrists flex backwards.

- Overhead diggers tense their fingers like blockers; setters have firm, but relaxed fingers.
- Overhead diggers use a quick elbow jab to dig; setters use their wrists to begin the setting motion.
- Overhead diggers can be flexible with their point of contact, moving it right or left; setters work to establish a consistent point of contact.

If coaches emphasize these critical differences, then balls will not blast through players who use this "big hands" technique for overhead digging. As a result, coaches could abandon the dreaded (and ineffective) "cupping" technique.

TIP 29: DON'T TEACH BLOCKING

I know that I'm in the minority on this one, but here goes. Most coaches want to teach blocking even when young/short players cannot get their palms over the net. Their rationale is that the earlier players learn the basic blocking eyework, footwork and handwork skills, the better they will be once they grow and/or begin to play at a higher level. These coaches want to be sure that they adequately prepare younger players for the future.

My thinking is a bit different. I don't want to teach blocking or any other skill that isn't necessary for my current team to be its very best. There are so many complex skills to teach beginners that impact winning and losing; why add skills that won't help us?

Of course, my detractors will point out that perhaps I over-emphasize winning. Well, I'll be the first one to admit that I like to win, and I believe that our players like to win, too. If winning didn't matter, we wouldn't keep score. However, I am a firm believer that all young players should get meaningful playing time in matches, so it's not that winning is my sole goal. I just believe I owe it to my players to help them be the best team they can be. If that means we practice serving and ace prevention and don't learn to block, then that's what we'll do.

There's another reason I'm anti-blocking for young players, and it's more philosophy-based. You often hear coaches complain that their players are poor decision makers, that they can't problem solve. Could it be that coaches are responsible for this? Many coaches teach the same exact systems to 11-year-old girls that our USA Men's National Team employs. The players, parents and coaches are all proud that they are learning these "advanced concepts" at such an early age.

I would argue that the system that is best for our USA men is not the best for our 11-year-old girls. Instead, let's teach our players a different system every year they play, a system that gives that individual team the best chance to win. Along with this, we teach the "why," so players understand that as they improve, the game changes, and different techniques and tactics are necessary. Now, we are coaching problem-solving, and our players' understanding of the game is much more flexible and nuanced. This makes so much more sense to me than the, "You'll need this later" approach.

Finally, in regards to the skill of blocking, I can teach many of the important concepts before a player ever jumps up to block. There is a ton of transfer in the basic skills we teach every young player. For example, blocking eyework is very similar to the reading skills we teach all defenders. Much (though not all) of the blocking footwork has similarities to our serve-receive and transition footwork, so these won't be foreign to our players as well. If we do a good job teaching overhead digging, then our young players will also have some blocking handwork skills.

So even though we haven't specifically taught blocking, our players are primed to learn the skill quickly. Furthermore, when the other team starts blasting balls that we cannot dig, the players will know the time is right to learn this important skill.

TIP 30: ONCE YOU'RE READY, TEACH BLOCKING AS A DEFENSIVE PROGRESSION

As I mentioned in the previous tip, when the opponent begins to hammer undiggable attacks, you'll know the time is right to teach blocking. When you do, integrating the blocking instruction into the general defensive philosophy makes the most sense.

Ironically, the first part of blocking instruction should be when NOT to block. I often observe young players mistakenly jumping to block against opponents' free balls. For us, that is an elementary mistake; lesson one is to only block attacks that we cannot easily dig. There's nothing worse than an opponent's "cupcake attack" that ends as a netting error or a ball that twizzles off the block for a kill.

Secondly, if we've done a good job teaching our floor defenders to read the line of attack, then we can transfer this concept to blocking. We therefore teach blockers to first ask, "Where is the set taking the hitter?" From there, blockers should place themselves in the line of this attack. Consequently, when we teach blocking, we try to do it against live hitters as much as possible. Though there are some good reasons to put attackers on boxes in blocker training, the more players can pick up cues from live hitters, the faster they will master this complex skill.

One of the mistakes I made earlier in my career was to begin blocking instruction with the admonition to "close the block." Now, all of the initial blocking instruction is done 1v1, blocker vs. hitter, so our blockers first learn the importance of intercepting the line of attack. We deal with closing the block later.

Here are our teaching keys for blocking:

- **Eyes:** Platform, Ball, Setter, Route, Ball, Hitter
- **Posture:** Flexed and athletic with elbows and hands inside the body line.
- **Small to big:** Though hands begin inside the shoulders, they become wider than the shoulders as they penetrate the plane of the net.
- **Slide over, slide back:** Players use a sliding motion with their hands, rather than a push and pull-back motion. We want to increase the time that the hands are over the plane of the net.
- **Transition:** Blockers land and immediately find the ball and run off the net.

And our favorite feedback includes:

- *LOA:* Intercept the line of attack.
- *See your hands:* Blocker's hands should stay in front of the head through the entire motion.
- *Steel pins:* Hands and fingers stay strong.
- *Get big:* Hands should take up space.

One recent improvement to our blocking instruction is the addition of the **Transition** key. We now practice transitioning whenever we practice blocking. We don't want to sacrifice transition practice in order to get more reps. We've made quality more important than quantity, so every time a ball passes the block, the blocker must find it, and take at least two steps off the net.

PART 4:
HOW DO I DESIGN AN EFFECTIVE PRACTICE?

TIP 31: BEGIN WITH BIG PICTURE PLANNING

I wouldn't consider organization to be my strong suit as a coach, but nevertheless, I strongly endorse the idea of a season practice plan. As a coach, you should spend the time to make a general outline of the different phases of each season and then note how the practices in each phase will differ. This helps you stay true to the "big picture" and not get sidetracked by the inevitable distractions that each season brings.

Here's an example of the general plan for my high school varsity team:

Phase 1: Tryouts and pre-competition
Given that we usually have small numbers, we can combine tryouts with early season training. In this phase, we emphasize: *Team Selection, Culture Building, Skills Training,* and

Introduction to Systems. This phase usually lasts 2-3 weeks. Approximately *20-30%* of our practice time is 6v6.

Phase 2: Pre-season competition (before league)
This is another 2-4 week phase that shifts to: *Systems Refinement, Skills Reinforcement, Culture in Competition* and *Role Clarification.* We usually play in at least 1-2 tournaments in this phase. Because our strengths and weaknesses get exposed at this point in the season, we often engage in a significant amount of experimentation. We might end up making major changes when it comes to systems and roles. Our 6v6 time in practice now increases to 40-50%.

Phase 3: League competition
This is the longest phase, and it usually lasts about five weeks. It will also include 1-2 tournaments. Because we are playing two league matches per week, we begin to take days off and shorten practice duration. We emphasize: *Culture Reinforcement, Systems Troubleshooting, Competing* and *Scouting.* In this phase, our 6v6 work exceeds 60% of our practice time.

Phase 4: Post-Season
This includes our county and state playoffs. It can last 1-4 weeks. In this final phase, we want to highlight: *Culture Celebration, Competing, Scouting* and *Minor Systems Tweaking.* We are now in 6v6 situations about 75% of our practice time.

You might notice that the one constant in each phase is *Culture.* I can't overestimate its importance for us. If we do a great job with our *Culture,* many of the other components will fall in line.

You'll also notice that I included our 6v6 training as a percentage of our practice time. Over the years, the amount of time I spend on 6v6 training has grown in every phase. After the second phase, I'm now much less skills-focused and much more team-focused. I believe this change has not only helped us improve at a faster rate but has also made practice more fun for our players.

TIP 32: ESTABLISH APPROPRIATE PRIORITIES FOR YOUR LEVEL

In Tip #7, I made the case for the importance of knowing the level of your team. This allows coaches to align their training priorities with the abilities of their players.

It isn't uncommon to see teams with misaligned priorities. An example is the beginning team that practices "1" (quick) sets before a competition. When the match begins, this team cannot serve-receive, so not only do they lose, they become disheartened by the lopsided 25-6 score. They run a single "1" during the match, and it results in an error. This is a classic misalignment story.

Here are some priorities to consider for each level:

Beginning team (over 50% of serves to this team result in aces):

- Movement and communication.
- Serving in.
- Ace prevention.

- Defensive rules of the road (opening up, parallel lines, etc.)
- Other skills training (in order): simple setting (mostly with platform), free ball offense (bumping over), platform digging and attacking over the net.
- Simple system – little to no specialization. (We'll get to systems in Part 5.)

Beginning/Intermediate team (30-50% of serves to this team result in aces):

- "Serving in" evolves to "serving tough."
- "Ace prevention" evolves to "passing to target on easy serves."
- Increase defensive range. Focus on reading, introduce floor moves and overhead digging.
- Add to skills training: setting, attacking to zones (off-speed), transition. Consider introducing blocking.
- Systems evolve: more specialization. Consider adding blocking to defensive system.

Intermediate/Advanced team (15-30% of serves to this team result in aces):

- First contact emphasis (serving and passing). Serving becomes more varied and strategic. Passing might now be more specialized.
- Skills refinement. More training is position-specific. Focus on efficiency and consistency.

- Defensive system development – blocking becomes a factor, and coordination of block and back row defense is necessary.
- Offensive system development – speed often becomes a factor in an effort to defeat the opponent's block. Coaches now differentiate in-system and out-of-system offense.
- Stats and analytics. Both self-scouting and scouting opponents.
- Strength training and injury prevention.

Advanced team (less than 15% of serves to this team result in aces):

- First contact. Serving and passing is always critical.
- Skills refinement. As the game becomes faster, efficient skill execution is critical.
- System enhancement. Teams might now employ multiple defenses and use a variety of offensive tactics to expose opponents' defensive weaknesses.
- Stats and analytics. These become more influential as the margins of winning/losing become thinner and thinner.
- Strength training, injury prevention, recovery. Given the demands of high-level volleyball, these become increasingly important.

Though these lists are far from complete, hopefully they will help you get a head start on establishing your priorities.

TIP 33: WISELY USE YOUR WARM-UP TIME

If we were to conduct a scientific study on "wasted practice time," we'd probably identify the first 15 minutes of most volleyball practices as the *most* wasteful. If your team practices for two hours, a 15-minute warm-up is 12.5% of your practice time. Given my nature, I like to put it in this competitive context, "Can our first 15 minutes of practice be better than all of our opponents'?"

Here are some do's and don'ts that might help your team make the best use of warm-up time:

Don't: *Take your eye off the clock.* For many teams, this 10-15 minute block expands to 20-25 minutes.

Do: *Chop the time in half, and set your watch alarm.* Let's take 7.5 minutes for our practice warm-up. Using random numbers (not 5 or 10) and half minutes sends a powerful message to your players that practice time is valuable.

Don't: *Static stretch.* The science doesn't support this, and neither does common sense. I don't understand how lying on the ground stretching gets you ready to play volleyball.

Do: *Play a game.* Immediately taking the floor and using the net to play a low-impact game – I like 3v3, no jumping, 2 contact – can both address a certain weakness and be fun. I like to emphasize communication in these first drills, so practice begins "sounding right." If you have multiple courts, maybe you can do setter training during this time as well.

Don't: *Jog.* If you don't want them to jog in a match, don't jog in practice.

Do: *VB Footwork.* Instead of jogging, better choices include step-shuffle passing footwork, attacking approaches or blocking footwork. These will raise the players' body temperature *and* help them become better at VB.

Don't: *Complete a complex series of dynamic stretching moves.* Though this is better than static stretching, and these choreographed moves might look cool, they have to pass the "VB relevancy" test.

Do: *Complete a short, simple series of dynamic moves that are relevant to volleyball.* These include lunges for leg strength, sprawls or other desired floor moves, and "dummy" arm swings (no ball).

Don't: *Let your players mindlessly spike balls into the ground.* I mentioned this earlier, but it bears repeating. This makes NO sense, and it's unbelievably pervasive at all levels. I limit my players to exactly three balls hit into the ground. I do this partly because it's good to have the ball in front of them when they hit, but mostly because they are so in love with this crazy ritual, I'm afraid they might mutiny if I were to ban it completely.

Do: *Warm up arms by hitting balls over the height of the net with shape and spin.* Begin at half speed and progress to full speed. This can be done with partners either over the net or without the net but pretending the net is between them.

Good luck with these. Not only will they help you make better use of the first minutes of practice, but they'll also better prepare your players for the rest of your practice session.

TIP 34: COMMUNICATE A CLEAR END TO EACH ACTIVITY

This is a critical concept for conducting effective, efficient practices. For new coaches, my message is simple, "For every activity in your practice plan, you should explain both the purpose and the criteria for completion."

Here are some popular ways to establish criteria to end a drill:

- **Time** – This is the most basic, and there are countless variations. "Ten minutes of serve-receive" is a start, but there are simple ways to make it better. Perhaps you designate three sessions of three minutes, each with a different focus. For skills work we do in pairs, we often use short time blocks (35 seconds). When time is up, players rotate partners, and I give them a new instruction.

- **Successful outcome** – An example might be, "We are going to pass 35 balls to target." The "outcome" could also be a skill key, such as, "We are going to pass-set-attack 20 balls using a four-step approach." At the outset, whether the ball goes in or out might not be part of this drill's criteria. It's all about the four-step approach.

Part 4: How Do I Design an Effective Practice?

- **Combine time and outcome** – "How many passes to target can we get in two minutes?" After one round, we can then try to top that number. We do have to be careful here. One mistake I've made is using this for individual serving. It resulted in players racing to serve as fast as possible, which is not what I wanted to encourage. My remedy was …

- **X out of 10**: "With 10 opportunities, how many times can you serve to Area 5?"

- **In-a-rows**: This works well with effort criteria such as, "We need to call the ball in serve-receive 20 times in a row." However, it can cause your players to be disheartened if you are overly optimistic. Telling your team, "We need to attack five in a row down the line to Area 1" doesn't seem too daunting, but many of my teams could easily get "stuck" here, and there's nothing worse than having to change the criteria because your team cannot achieve it. A safer approach is to combine it with time, such as, "What's the highest in-a-row we can achieve in two minutes?"

- **Competition**: A simple competitive game could pit team vs. team or player vs. player. I like shorter games rather than longer, so we might begin a game at 20-20 rather than 0-0. If you play best of 3 or best of 5 games beginning at 20-20, your team practices a bunch of end-of-game situations.

We haven't spent much time talking about coaching toys, but this tip brings to mind two of my favorites. The first is a scoreboard, and the second is a clock. You can use both to help players stay focused on the task.

TIP 35: BALANCE ROUTINE WITH VARIETY

One way to evaluate this tip is to imagine the two opposites. That is, think about running the same practice over and over. You would benefit from the efficient use of time; there would be no need to explain how to run a drill or play a particular game. The team would move seamlessly from activity to activity and probably become very accomplished in certain phases of the game. Of course, you'd run the risk of players losing interest due to the monotony, and the possibility of them "going through the motions."

Or you might imagine practices that emphasize variety. These sessions challenge players with new, creative activities the coach designs to target a team's specific weaknesses. Players might be more invested in such practices, but there's an efficiency problem. In each session, the players spend an inordinate amount of time learning the new activities. Coaches talk a lot in these sessions, and players are often learning more about drills than about how to improve their play.

The obvious answer is combining the two, using both routine and variety to create the most enriching practice environment. Here are five ways to do it:

1. **Employ a different practice template for each phase of your season.** I mentioned the season organization concept back in Tip #31. By dividing your season into parts, you can establish routine in each particular phase and also get

some variety by making changes to your practice template in each new phase.

2. **Alternate areas of emphasis.** I continue to play around with this idea. I've designated defensive and offensive practices, and I've also split offense into in-system and out-of-system, and defense into at-the-net and off-the-net. We can run the same drills/games for each but do them in alternating practices.

3. **Take your daily vitamins.** Some activities are so fundamental to our success that we do them every day. For my middle school teams, warm-up footwork (serve-receive step-shuffles, and approaches), a serving progression and a defensive pursuit drill are part of every practice. These are relatively short in duration (2-7 minutes), but we get better by doing them every practice.

4. **Add competition days.** This is an idea from former Stanford coach John Dunning, and it's a great one. Every five practices, he throws out his normal practice template, and his team puts on uniforms, does a pre-match warm-up and plays. Because he wants his team to start fast in matches, he simulates that in practice.

5. **Play the same game but modify the rules or scoring.** I saved the best for last, and this is one I'm constantly refining. For example, I frequently will vary my favorite 4v4 game, Kamikaze. (The traditional way to play is with two players at the net in LF and RF and two in the backcourt in LB and RB. It's a back row setter game, so the back row player must set unless there's an emergency – like a low

dig to the net. Attackers attack from the front row vs. one blocker. When a team scores two points, another team rotates in to replace the losing team.) We vary Kamikaze in the following ways:

- *Warm-up Game:* Downball, rotate after each crossing.
- *Chase:* Initiate hard-driven ball to create scramble out-of-system set.
- *LB Setting:* Initiate to setters in RB, so LB (libero and serving MB) practice out-of-system setting.
- *Tooling & Coverage:* Add players to the front row, so instead of hitting 1v1, attackers face 2 or 3 blockers.
- *Serve-Receive:* One team (primary passers) stays on, and the challenging team rotates through. Challengers are always serving.

Finally, the use of routine will help make practice planning easier. You don't need a ton of new activities. Re-use your favorites and add a little twist to make them more interesting/challenging.

TIP 36: WHEN POSSIBLE, TURN DRILLS INTO GAMES

One of the most important concepts in practice design is "transfer," meaning coaches want all their practice activities to transfer to the game. This explains the push for more "random" game-like training and the subsequent reduction of "blocked" training.

Here's an example. Thirty years ago, if I wanted my OH's to improve their ability to hit down the line, I would design a simple "blocked" drill that looked something like this: I toss sets and a group of three hitters attack until they hit 15 total to a targeted area down the line. Though this drill might allow for a large number of opportunities in a short amount of time, there are some "transfer" issues. In matches, hitters don't do the following:

- Begin in the same exact spot.
- Hit perfect tosses coming from the same location.
- Attack with no blockers.

Consequently, my pretty little line hitting drill does not benefit my players much once the competition starts. It lacks transfer.

Today, I might design the following games to teach OH line attacking. We begin playing two simultaneous games of *Long-court Doubles* on a single court. An antenna at the midpoint along the net divides the court lengthwise. For the first 3 minutes, we play "downball" style with no jumping, no blocking and no scoring. Players focus on ball contact and controlling the ball in the narrow court. Next, we open it up and let players jump to attack, block and keep score. After 3 minutes, the winning team moves "up" a court, and the losing team moves down. Players switch partners and play again.

Of course, these long-court games may be an improvement over my blocked drill, but they have some transfer issues as well. In matches, most digs and sets are not limited to a narrow court, and outside hitters commonly hit against 2 blockers, not one.

So after the long-court games, we'll play a 6v6 game with some adjusted scoring. Normal points are still scored, but *any attack down the line* is worth a bonus point, and a *kill down the line* (or tool off the line blocker) is worth 3 bonus points. Finally, to encourage players to take some risks, we will replay any ball hit down the line that goes out of bounds.

There you have it. Your challenge is to combine the science of coaching (random rather than blocked activities) with the art of coaching (creative drill design that turns drills into games).

TIP 37: BECOME AN MC (MASTER OF CONSTRAINTS)

As demonstrated in the previous tip, addressing a team weakness with a "blocked" drill is not too difficult. If my team can't hit down the line, I can throw up a bunch of balls and tell them to hit line. However, experienced coaches know that this training often doesn't transfer. They must design some targeted games, creating a better learning environment that transfers to competition.

There's a movement in motor learning that supports this concept, and it's called *Constraints Led Coaching*. Here is my elementary definition: *Play volleyball, but add some rules (constraints) that encourage players to figure out how to win.* In the process, they address a particular area of the game that you want to improve.

The two main categories of constraints are the *environment* and the *task*. I explained *Long-court Doubles* (one of my favorites) in the last tip, and that's a classic example of an environmental constraint. I simply changed the size of the court. Other examples include changing the net height, putting a sheet over the net (to accentuate vision), or allowing play off the walls (to encourage pursuit).

Constraining the task is much more common, and this includes any kind of scoring alteration. Plus/minus points for certain behaviors is often an effective way to focus players' attention, especially those who are competitive and want to win.

When I work with beginning players, my favorite task constraint is *"Two Contacts."* We simply play volleyball, but each side is limited to 2 contacts rather than 3. You'll notice a bunch of good stuff when your team plays this game. First, players get more opportunities and more rallies. With only 2 contacts, there are less opportunities for them to mess up, so they are successful far more often. Secondly, it's faster. Beginners' volleyball with 3 contacts and a bunch of errors is painfully slow. Limiting it to 2 contacts speeds it up significantly. Finally, they play the types of random balls they encounter in competitions. It's strange to watch a novice group trying to spike before a game when they haven't yet learned how to bump a free ball over the net. *Two-Contacts* solves this problem.

Two-Contacts works best with inexperienced groups but has benefits for more advanced teams as well. Playing this game with experienced players will spotlight out-of-system offense, communication and decision-making, and free ball and down ball transition.

Give it a try, no matter what level you coach. You'll be well on your way to becoming an accomplished MC.

TIP 38: USE HALF-AND-HALF DRILLS TO SET HIGH STANDARDS

Though my practices have evolved and lean strongly toward random, game-like activities, I'm still an old-timer who believes there's a time and place for some "blocked" drills, especially when coaching beginning players.

My staple format for blocked drills are "Half and Half" drills. Half the team is involved in the drill, and the other half is feeding, shagging and counting. The first key to these drills is "single-item focus." That is, the drill will challenge players to change a particular behavior. The second key is that the first time a player doesn't change the behavior, that group loses its opportunity, and the two halves switch.

Here is an example. Coaches of beginning teams often ask me how to better teach communication. We use a simple drill named *"Call It."* It begins easy, with 3 lines of passers. I'm on the opposite side, rapidly firing balls in order to RB, MB and LB. To remain in the drill, each player in the group must call the ball before it crosses the net – loudly enough for an old man (me) to hear it. I'm a stickler for "Mine," but for some it's a bit too militaristic. If "I go" or "Me, me, me" works for you, that's great. We set the clock for a minute, and I start feeding like a madman. The first time someone doesn't call it, we stop and the groups switch. The first group that makes it for the entire minute wins.

For a more experienced team, we can still put 3 players out, but now it's a pass-set-hit-cover rendition of *Call It.* One player "calls it" and passes, another "calls it" and sets and the third "calls for a certain set" and then attacks. Finally, the two non-attackers must call, "Cover, cover, cover" after the ball is set. Once again, as soon as one player in the sequence doesn't call it, that half of the team is out, and the other half tries to complete a minute of diligent communication.

The cool thing about these half-and-half drills is that I do not nag and complain (two of my more endearing traits). I simply set the criteria, and if it's not met, I smile and say, "Bye-bye. Switch!" Instead of me doing it, players begin to remind each other. Of course, our competitive players learn exactly who is liable to mess up, so they station themselves in line next to the culprit in order to provide a gentle reminder before the play.

Besides simple communication criteria, we also use these drills for technique work such as passers angling their platform to target or blockers and defenders following proper eye sequence. Any behavior that you are looking to change can be the single-item focus of the drill. We've had some success with this format, and I hope you do as well.

TIP 39: PUT YOUR ASSISTANT(S) TO WORK

Thinking back to my early coaching days, I had no clue how much my teams could improve if I did a better job of coaching my assistant coaches. Of course, I've coached plenty of teams by myself, and this tip might not apply to coaches who always fly solo. However, if you're fortunate enough to have someone to give you a hand, it can have a significant impact on your team.

Here are four specific tasks that every worthy assistant should master.

1. **Be a "copycat."** Simply, the assistant will do the same exact task that the head coach is doing, but now the team is in two small groups instead of one big one. I see so many drills that could be twice as good if the head coach would give up a bit of control and trust the assistant to guide half the team. If your team gets twice as many reps, they are going to be better, quicker.

2. **Be a "pullout tutor."** One of the most common complaints I hear from coaches is about the discrepancy in talent on their teams. Often a team has one or two players who are significantly less experienced and less skilled. These players often slow the pace, and when you stop play to instruct them, it often frustrates your most talented players. The simple remedy is the assistant pulling this player (or two) out for individual instruction. You get to move at a faster pace with the team, and the weak players get the individual attention and instruction they so desperately need. It's a win-win! Oh, I forgot. Your assistant is no longer holding up the net support and is now making a valuable contribution. It's a win-win-win.

3. **Be a stat master.** When I mention "master" here, I'm not talking about being a stat expert. It's merely mastering a couple of simple stats that make a difference at your level. Once you give your assistant or assistants the parameters, they can not only develop a system for taking the stats but also work with you to decide how to best share them with the players.

   If you coach a beginning group, you might believe that you're not ready for stats. I disagree. What if your assistant kept two stats in practice? The first is successful serves in a row by each individual player. The second is each individual's in-a-row contacts in serve-receive that do NOT result in an ace. Over time, both of these numbers should increase, so it's fun for your players to see their individual improvement. It's also fun to see who sets the standard on your team and then who makes the biggest gains. By keeping and sharing a few simple stats, your assistant can become a motivational genius.

4. **Play the role of "COGSS,"** *Catcher of Good Specific Stuff.* On any team, there is so much good stuff that goes unnoticed, especially with technique and off-the-ball effort. The secret is to divide and conquer. Maybe you put your assistant in charge of coverage and transition while you are working with setter and hitter decision-making. You might also instruct the assistant to only be positive – that is, only recognize players who transition and cover aggressively. This not only reinforces critical off-the-ball skills, but it also enhances the practice vibe. The positive feedback keeps the smiles coming. Once again, now the assistant is making a meaningful impact.

Of course, not every assistant can master all four roles, but if you spend a bit of time, any assistant can become competent in at least one or two. Most important, once you demonstrate to assistants how they can positively influence the team, they quite often "catch the bug." Now we have another passionate coach in our midst. How great is that!

TIP 40: REMEMBER THE F-WORDS

If you told me that you only had time to read one tip in this Effective Practice section, it would be this one. The tip is quite simple, "Make it fast, and make it fun." Here are five ways to do it:

1. **Throw-ins** – Nothing slows down practice like a string of missed serves. Our remedy is to always have a player or coach prepared to immediately throw in another ball. As far as scoring, if the serving team wins the throw-in, it's a wash (replay). That way the receiving team always earns its points.

2. **Keep lines short** – If there are ever more than 3-4 players in a single line, that's a problem and the drill needs to be re-worked. A few simple ways include splitting the team into two groups instead of one, adding a defensive element (a one-way drill becomes two-way), or adding a fundamentals station. Whatever the solution, keeping players active is key!

3. **Use short time durations** – In the old days, I was guilty of trying to "toughen up" teams by keeping them in drills

until they succeeded. No more. I can get the same benefit by using shorter time durations, then repeating them. Instead of one 10-minute activity that stretches 25-35 minutes due to poor play, I now stop it after 10 minutes. We will break it up with 2 minutes of serving, and then maybe go back for another 10 minutes to see if we can make improvements.

4. **Keep the games short** – Though games (or sets, if you like the newer terminology) are to 25 in matches, we rarely play to 25 in practice. Any lopsided game is an energy-sapper, so we'll play best out of five games starting at 20-20. If the games aren't competitive, I can always juggle the players or change the rules. The short games keep players more engaged.

5. **Talk less, smile more** – "Feedback on the fly" is a staple for us, meaning that coaches can communicate (catch them doing it RIGHT) while the ball is in play. If we do stop it, I'll have an assistant calling out the time in 20 second increments; 30 seconds is my target. Finally, if we focus on catching positive models, both the coaches and players end up having much more fun.

There you have it. Hopefully, you found a few nuggets of value in this section that will help you run more effective practices. Time to get started on systems.

PART 5:
WHAT'S A SYSTEM, AND HOW MANY DO I NEED?

TIP 41: REMEMBER ROBIN SHARMA

Though it's on my reading list, I haven't yet read Robin Sharma's book, *The Monk Who Sold His Ferrari*. Even more than his catchy title, I love Mr. Sharma's popular quote, **"Simplicity is the trademark of genius."** As we begin to explore volleyball systems, please remember this adage. Volleyball skills are challenging to learn and master, so when it comes to systems, coaches should make the game easier for players rather than more difficult.

Let me explain. The two most common offensive systems for Intermediate-Advanced and Advanced teams are the 5-1 and the 6-2. The first number signifies the number of hitters, and the second the number of setters. So in a 5-1, a single setter sets in all six rotations. In a 6-2, the two setters will be opposite of each other in the rotation, and they will set when they are in the back row and hit when they rotate to the front row.

Now let's create a little hypothetical situation. We are coaching against each other at the Beginning level. Our teams are identical in talent. The only difference between the two squads is that you are a Robin Sharma fan, and I am not acquainted with him.

We both have 10 hours of practice time before we play each other. You spend almost all of your time working on serving and ace prevention. You have to teach some kind of offensive system, so you spend a measly 10% of your time teaching an elementary 6-6, with the player in MF facing and setting either RF or LF (no back-setting).

In the other gym, I am hard at work getting my players to understand the 6-2. I believe that it provides wonderful advantages to our team, since my best two players can set in the back row and hit in the front row. Though I plan to spend about 20% of my time teaching the system, I find that the 6-2 and its switching and transition complexities take much longer than I expected. I end up spending nearly 80% of the time teaching the 6-2, and as competition approaches, most of my players are still confused.

Game time! Needless to say, your team wins, and sadly for my squad, it's not even close. My players can neither serve in nor prevent your "bullies" from serving long runs of aces. The first set ends 25-8, and though the second is a bit better on the scoreboard for me (25-13), it's actually worse because you are able to give significant time to your weakest players and I'm trying to preserve a bit of the team's dignity, so my weakest players are barely playing. In addition, we let several easy balls drop because players are in the process of "switching." I spend the whole match telling players where to stand,

and their confusion (and mine!) is obvious to everyone. It gets worse. Because we can't serve-receive, my two "stars" are upset because they rarely have opportunities to set or attack, and I don't know who is more agitated, their parents or those of our weakest players.

There are several lessons here, but as we get into the following system work, the crucial one is to remember Robin Sharma. Just as important, remember my corresponding corollary, "Complexity is the trademark of foolishness."

TIP 42: CHOOSE SYSTEM EVOLUTION OVER PLUG AND PLAY

The situation in Tip #41 is an example of what I call "Plug and Play." That is, coaches have a particular system in mind, and they plug players into the system. These systems are often copies of those employed by experienced high school, college or professional teams. The rationale is that if players learn these complex systems early, they will be better prepared for high-level volleyball.

Many middle school, freshmen and JV coaches employ these complex systems because they're "preparing players for varsity." Consequently, you'll often see lower-level teams choose systems that inhibit their abilities rather than enhancing them. These teams will mistakenly:

- Employ back row setters in a 6-2.
- Serve-receive with three players.

- Stand at the net to block even if they cannot reach over the net.
- Specialize positions in the front row and back row.

Rather than selecting an advanced system that is a bad fit and hoping players grow into it, let's begin with a simple system and then allow it to evolve over the course of a season. This has three significant advantages over "Plug and Play." The first is that it makes volleyball easier to learn. Beginners are going to struggle with the skills, so the easier we make the rest of it, the better. Secondly, they will play better. They will attend to keeping the ball off the floor and not to where they should go to switch positions.

Most important, they will learn about the "Why?" I often hear coaches complain that players can't problem-solve, that they have to be told everything. For players coming out of "Plug and Play," this shouldn't be surprising. Coaches have instructed them to do senseless tasks from day one.

Let me elaborate. I absolutely hate the 6-2 for Beginning or even Beginning-Intermediate teams. We know these teams will struggle in serve-receive, so it makes no sense to run a setter out of the back row. If the pass is low, the setter won't get there. If it's high and tight to the net, the setter can't knock it over (back row violation). For passes that are 10 feet off the net, there will be confusion between the setter and the attackers. Finally, if RB has to set, our RB defense will suffer. Despite these obvious disadvantages, I see all sorts of inexperienced teams struggling in a 6-2.

Here's a better way to teach an offensive system using the evolutionary approach:

1. Begin with a 6-6, with whoever is in MF setting. This allows the players to first learn how to rotate.
2. Quickly progress to a 4-2, designating a front row setter and switching her to MIDDLE front. (See Tip #43.)
3. Progress to a 6-3. Instead of having just two setters, use three. "We think our setters might be good attackers, so let's give them a chance to hit." Separate the three setters in the rotation, and each of them will attack when playing LF and then set in the MF and RF spots.
4. If you need to add a middle blocker to stop an opponent's attack, move your setter to RF.
5. Progress to using a back row setter – but only on free balls. The passing will be better than in serve-receive or transition; your setter will have more time to get to the target area, and she won't need to worry about defending RB. It's the painless way to teach back row setting.

During this evolutionary process, players learn the logical reason to progress to the next step. They take pride in both their improved skills and the shiny new offensive system that takes advantage of these skills. The takeaway is obvious. Stay away from "Plug and Play"!

TIP 43: DELAY SPECIALIZATION

Don't get me started!

I'll begin with a short anecdote, and maybe then you'll feel my pain. A few years ago, I ran a summer clinic for beginning players. They were in middle school, and it was a LOW-level group.

So we were teaching the attack approach, and everything was splendid until we began hitting live sets from both LF and RF. When one of the 12-year-olds ran under the ball on her RF attack, I tried to help her with spacing. Her response was, "I'm an outside hitter. I don't hit here." What?!!!

This girl can barely serve over the net, cannot serve-receive at all, and plays little to no defense. The only thing she knows about playing volleyball is that she's an OH, and she doesn't have to worry about anything that might not relate specifically to that position. What have we done?

Let's get back to Robin Sharma and keep it simple. Let's teach kids to not let the ball land in our box and to hit it somewhere in the other box that makes it difficult for the opponent.

We should spend our time teaching these two fundamental concepts, and delay specialization for as long as possible. Encourage the tall kids to pass, set and play defense, and make the short kids attack. For young/inexperienced teams that don't block, the only positions should be setter and non-setter. When it's time to block, I suggest blocking the entire net with a single blocker. Then the positions are setter, hitter and blocker. When you encounter attackers that can easily score against your single block, then and only then will it be time to specialize front row positions.

I know it's difficult to teach the game like this, since many critics will foolishly accuse you of "holding back" your athletes. Put in the earplugs and do it anyway!

As a high school coach of a fairly successful program, I don't want OH's and opposites, I want volleyball players. If they can serve, pass, play defense and hit it with heat into the box, they have a spot on the team. Based on our needs, I will assign them a position and teach them the intricacies.

TIP 44: BEGIN AT THE BEGINNING – SERVE AND SERVE-RECEIVE

The first three tips in this section address a coach's general approach to system development. Now it's time to begin the process. Though most coaches will start with the offensive system (4-2, 5-1, 6-2), I like to put first things first. There's no need to worry about setters and attackers if you first can't serve and serve-receive.

Many coaches don't think of serving as a system that needs attention, but I do. It's a simple system with only a single variable - serving order. As a coach, you decide the order; the lower the level, the more important the decisions. For Beginning teams, a simple rule is to rank your top six servers and put them in that order. That seems easy enough, but what if your two setters are far and away your two best servers? Do you put them at the top of the serving order, or do you keep them opposite each other in the rotation so now one of them will be your fourth rather than your second server? There are no perfect answers here, but at the lower levels, I would probably prioritize serving over setting.

Coaches should also create a comprehensive serve-receive system BEFORE dealing with any setting or attacking concerns. These are the questions you should tackle:

- How many passers will we use in serve-receive?

- What is our formation, and how can I help my passers begin in the same spot every time?
- What are the rules of the road? That is, what happens when balls are served in seams?
- Is every passer "equal," or will we put our best passers in positions to receive more serves?
- What adjustments will we make when we struggle?
- Does the formation allow the setter to begin in the target area or to easily get there?

Once again, coaches should address these before any setting or attacking decisions. Below is the serve-receive system that I developed for our low-level middle school club program:

- We pass with five in every rotation. We pass high and off the net.
- We are in a W formation. LF and RF begin at "1 and 1," one step behind the 10-foot line and one step in from the sideline. Middle back (MB) is in the middle of the court, one big step behind the line of LF and RF (about 15 to 16 feet from the net). RB and LB are centered "in the gaps" between the front row and MB players. They are a half step deeper than MB.

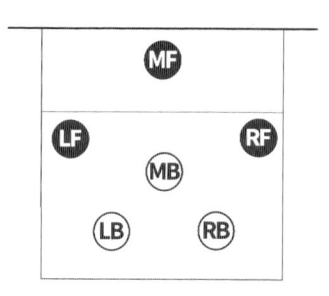

- LF and RF rules: They can only pass balls "in their core." That is, no lateral passing, since a back row player can get behind that ball. On any deep ball, open up outside the court and call "Deep!"
- Middle back rules: Mid-back is the toughest position. Like the front-row passers, middle backs must have their core behind the ball (no lateral passing). On deep balls, middle backs open up and DEEPEN to the opposite side of the ball. For instance, if the ball is between the middle back player and the right back and the RB is going to take it, the middle back opens up to the left and slides deeper into the court, creating a clear path between the passer and setter. This also keeps the middle back from interfering with the setter's pursuit of the pass.
- RB and LB rules: "Ball goes, you go." These players will always back up the front row passer or middle back. Because they are in deep positions, they are the only passers allowed to lateral pass.
- Parallel lines and seams rules: LF and RF go in front of MB, and MB goes in front of LB and RB. For balls between players, whoever gets behind it first takes it.

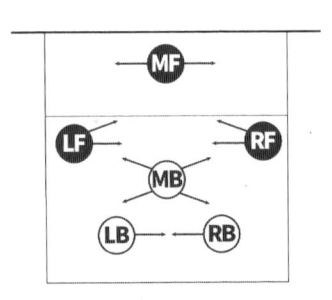

- In the developmental phase, every passer is equal. Everyone learns all the passing spots. Against extra tough servers, LF and RF move back so they are even with middle back. We call this formation "5 flat."

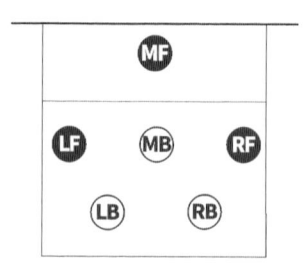

```
           MF

     LF    MB    RF

        LB    RB
```

We always have front row setters in serve-receive, so setter penetration is never an issue.

Of course, this five person W formation has advantages (simple court coverage, no overlap issues) and disadvantages (more seams and no specialization). As players and teams improve, evolving to a 3-4 person formation that puts your best passers in position to receive the most serves is probably a prudent move. Now that we have a pass in the air, we can start with the offense.

TIP 45: FIND SOME SETTERS AND PUT THEM IN MIDDLE FRONT

This tip is generally directed to coaches of inexperienced teams, but I used a MF setter for part of last season with an advanced high school group. We had only two "real" middle hitters (MH's) on our team, and when we lost one to an injury, our 6-0 All-League setter was the best option to play MH. She was great! She loved that there was no congestion in transition (no MH to avoid), and she embraced using the dump as our quick attack and coupling it with tempo balls to the pins.

But I digress. This tip is for coaches of young and/or inexperienced teams that are not yet blocking. If you are in that situation, put your setter in MF rather than RF. There are many advantages:

- It's a simple target area for your passers. It's easier to pass to the middle than pass to the right.
- There's less congestion for your setter since the middle is clear of any attacker.
- Your setter has more range for balls in the court. When balls are shanked left, the MF setter will get to balls that RF will not.
- There's no confusion with attackers. A set from RF will often land between the MF and LF attackers, causing confusion. In MF, the setter can either face RF or LF, so attacker confusion is eliminated.
- It also makes it easy to set a pipe to the middle back. Without a MF attacker, there's no congestion.
- MF setting is a great position for your best athlete. She can patrol the net, dump tight passes, and attack overpasses and oversets. For athletes on low-level teams who are hesitant to set because they'd rather hit, I give them this sage advice, "You'll get far more "good" sets from the opposition than we'll be able to give you…."

- In baseball, the pitcher, catcher and shortstop are key positions because they are in the middle of the field. The MF setter is the perfect volleyball analogy; it's where the action is.

Once our opponents begin to attack balls that we can't dig, we will begin to block. At that time, I usually switch the setter to RF and put a blocker in MF. The only exception is when my setter is one of my best blockers. In this scenario, I keep her in the middle and simply teach her how to block.

Before wrapping up, let's talk about a creative solution we employed a couple of years ago when I had only one setter on my low-level 14s team. We played a 5-1, but our setter's base position in all six rotations was MF. Our front row setter rotations were the same, but we had to learn a new back row alignment. When the setter was in the back row, we always switched her to middle back and then "inverted" her with MF. So in three rotations, our MF attacker played middle back and only hit pipes. Our setter had to remember that she couldn't dump from over the net height in the back row rotations, but she was a quick study. That little team was pretty efficient in that wacky system. It remains one of my all-time favorites.

Give the MF setter a try. Trust me, you'll love it.

TIP 46: DETOUR – TEACH YOUR PLAYERS ABOUT ATTACKING EFFICIENCY

Before we get into offense and attacking, we need to take a short detour.

If you take a peek at a college volleyball box score, you will notice that along with the individual game scores, there's a number included that looks like a baseball batting average. You'll also notice that the team with the higher average usually wins the game.

This number is the team's *attacking efficiency*, and there is a good reason that it's now included in a prominent place in every box score. It's the most impactful stat on winning and losing.

To calculate *attacking efficiency,* you take a player's (or team's) kills, subtract errors, and divide by total attacks. For example, if a player has 5 kills and 2 errors on 10 attacks, she is hitting .300, (5-2)/10.

As far as benchmarks are concerned, a good goal is .300, but .200 is OK. .100 is mediocre, and hitting negative (more errors than kills) is a major problem. As the level improves, MA's generally hit for higher percentages than OH's since MA's usually attack in-system, while OH's have to deal with a ton of out-of-system opportunities.

This is an important stat because your players' numbers will help you make important decisions regarding your offensive system. Simply, you will want your most efficient attackers to have the most attempts. We'll get to the nuts and bolts of this in Tip #48.

The takeaway here is that your players should know the method to your madness. If you are using *attacking efficiency* to make decisions on set distribution, then you should teach them the simple formula. It's only fair that they know how you evaluate them. I take the time to teach *attacking efficiency* to all my teams, even the young ones. Some critics – I have many – might counter that focusing on such analytics for young players could hinder their development or damage their self-esteem. I would argue that they are graded every day at school; they are very accustomed to a variety of analytics and evaluation. It's only damaging if we don't clearly explain how we are evaluating them.

Once you teach your attackers the simple formula, they will begin to grasp the importance of "managing risk." That is, if there is little to no chance for a kill, players shouldn't risk making an error. Following this simple rule will allow you to differentiate "good" attacking errors (good set, good alignment, hit hard and just out) vs. "bad" attacking errors (bad set and/or bad alignment, ball hit in the bottom of net or out by 15 feet).

For developing teams, once you get a handle on ace prevention, eliminating "bad" attacking errors is your next challenge. In competitions at this level, if the serve-pass battle is even, managing risk often becomes the crucial variable that determines the winner.

TIP 47: DETOUR #2 – ALSO TEACH THEM ABOUT THE FALLACY OF STATISTICS

I have had the good fortune to work with the same assistant coach for over 30 years. DJ is not only the most curious man in America, he is also the nicest. Players love him, and he brings sunshine in the gym each and every day. This provides a nice balance for our team, since my disposition can occasionally turn stormy.

DJ also teaches math, is among the most well-read folks I know, and is a dear friend. One of his favorite sayings (stolen from Mark Twain, I believe) is, "Nothing lies like a statistic." There is a bit of irony here, since one of DJ's primary responsibilities is taking stats.

I suggested in the last tip that we teach our players about *attacking efficiency*. It's a critical statistic when it comes to designing and evaluating an offense. However, like any statistic, it doesn't tell the whole story, and it's worth the time and effort to teach your players how to think critically.

Here is the example I use. Once players understand *attacking efficiency*, I ask them this simple question, "Are all .300 hitters equally valuable to the team?" This seems like a simple question, and they usually answer in the affirmative. Then I write out some attacking stats on the whiteboard.

In 10 attempts, both Player A and Player B have 3 kills and no errors. They both hit .300. However, of the 7 "in-play" attacks, Player A hit 7 "cupcakes" to the opponent's libero, and after a perfect in-system dig, they scored easily. Our team lost all seven of those points.

On the other hand, Player B was able to keep the opponent out-of-system on her 7 "in-play" attacks. She hit at the back row setter, tipped at the ace attacker, and chopped a couple down the line that were barely kept in play. We ended up winning 6 of those 7 points.

At the end of the day, when Player A attacked, we won 3 out of 10 points. When Player B attacked, we won 9 out of 10. Those two .300 hitters do not look so similar anymore.

Now our players begin to understand DJ's wise admonition, and they also learn that their coaches will look beyond the numbers to identify and reward each player's unique contribution. Enough of the stat talk. Let's get back to offensive systems.

TIP 48: ON OFFENSE, SET YOUR MOST EFFICIENT ATTACKERS

This seems obvious, but there are three common roadblocks that prevent coaches from following this bit of common sense. The first is when the coach doesn't have a firm grasp of attacker ranking. That's what makes *attacking efficiency* stats so important. Without them, coaches might be deceived when it comes to ranking attackers. A player who has dynamic kills but makes several "bad" errors might be overvalued. You might remember the impressive attacks and forget the errors. On the other end of the spectrum, a less dynamic attacker might get "cheap" kills, but if she's error-free, she might be more valuable than you think. Keeping this one stat will give you clarity when you decide who should receive the most sets.

The second roadblock is a big one – system incompatibility. Let me explain. Once you get a good idea of who should receive the most sets, you now have to develop an offensive system that makes it easy to set those players. Let's say you have two attackers who are significantly better than their teammates. A simple system might be to put these two in the OH position and then set them a bunch of balls. To make it easy for your setter, you might decide to pass to a target 5 to 10 feet off the net, right in the middle of the court. This system would be a compatible one; it's designed to get the ball to your best attackers.

Let's look at a slightly different scenario. What if these two attackers are your only blockers, and they have to be MA's? Maybe you are also enamored with a quick offense, so you want to set these players a "1" set in the middle. Both of them can crush it. Now we are venturing toward incompatibility. In order to set a "1," the pass has to be near perfect, so unless your team's ball control is extraordinary, you won't be able to set your best attackers as often as you'd like. A remedy would be to abandon your fascination with speed, change the target area to far right, and set a bunch of "2" sets in the middle of the court. Now we're back to a compatible system.

The third and final roadblock is setter malfunction. After you've identified your best attackers and then designed a system to get them the ball, one important task remains – setter tactics training. Common problems include setters who feed their friends, those who dish every hitter an equal amount of sets, or those who set the nearest hitter. Making sure that you and your setter are aligned is the final piece of the offensive puzzle.

Early in the season, I sit down with our setter(s) and together we review our *attacking efficiency* stats from practice, both individual and as a team. I explain that *team attacking efficiency* is one way to evaluate a setter's effectiveness in each match. Then I ask the big question: "To be our best, what should our set distribution look like at the end of the match?" The setter might come up with something that looks like this: "Our top attacker should receive 35-38% of the sets. Our next three attackers are about the same, so they should each get about 15% of the sets. I'll dump about 10%, and then sprinkle the other 10% to whoever is hot." We will then review each rotation and formulate a plan of attack that is in harmony with our set distribution goals.

After each match, we'll meet again to review our individual and team *attacking efficiency* numbers. We'll also look at set distribution. For low-level teams, we might just check that we are setting enough balls to our best attackers. For higher-level teams, we'll evaluate the setter's success in getting her best attackers "good looks." That is, the setter should be able to create opportunities so our top hitters face fewer blockers and/or weaker blockers than our opponents would want.

So there you have the simple offensive recipe for success: efficient attackers, a compatible system and a perceptive setter. Time for defense!

TIP 49: USE COMMON SENSE TO POSITION YOUR DEFENDERS

There's that old saying that common sense is not so common, so I will start our defensive system discussion with some good old common sense. Here we go:

- A volleyball court is a 30 x 30-foot box, so it's 900 square feet. With six players on the floor, and if we evenly divide responsibilities, each player should defend approximately 150 square feet.
- If players can't execute a big enough block to defend their 150 square feet, they should not block.
- If players do not block, there is no great reason to assign them base positions on the net.
- Position diggers in the spots where the most balls land. It also makes more sense to cover the middle of the court than the perimeters, since the perimeter shots are riskier.
- The less movement between "base" (starting) and "release to dig" positions, the better.
- If we teach players to both platform dig and overhand dig, we can improve their digging range.

As you might have noticed by my not-so-subtle overtures, I'm not a big fan of blocking until it becomes absolutely necessary. For me, "absolutely necessary" means the other team is attacking a fair number of balls that we can't possibly dig.

My aversion to blocking has several causes. First, it's hard to teach and learn, since the feedback loop is so random. (You can form a perfect block, but if the attacker "fluffs" a ball over it for a kill, no one knows.) In addition, too many bad things can happen. It starts with net violations and tools, and also includes transition complications. If your best attacker is blocking in RF, it's very difficult to set her.

Since there are plenty of places to learn about "normal" defensive systems with blocking, I'm going to focus on systems with no blocking or limited blocking. We'll start with no blocking systems:

1. Use a W formation with the same positions/responsibilities that we outlined for SR in Tip #44. The two differences on defense are the MF (5 feet off the net) is defending rather than preparing to set, and the middle back defender is one huge step closer to the net (12-15 feet).

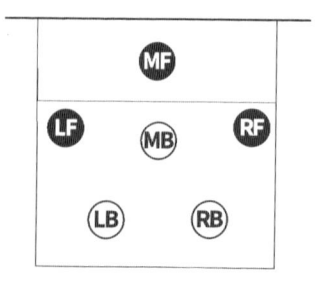

2. Communication, parallel lines and opening up rules are exactly the same as in SR (see Tip #44). The principal difference is that an attacked ball will come quicker than a serve since it doesn't have to travel 30+ feet before it reaches the defenders.

3. Defend the ball that lands the fastest. Players are responsible for balls in front of them.

Here are a few ways to evolve into a blocking system taking baby steps:

1. Use one blocker to block the entire net, and situate the other five defenders around the block.

2. Depending on their relative skill, allow some pin blockers to block and others to pull off the net to cover tips. When one of our 6-2 setters went on a college visit, we ran a 5-1 with our 5-foot-1 setter and simply pulled her off the net. I thought we would be punished by the other team's talented LF's, but they had trouble scoring. Their attackers even made some uncharacteristic errors trying to sharpshoot down the line. Blocking wasn't nearly as important as I thought.

3. "Dedicate" your middle blocker to one pin. (This is known as "trap blocking.") As offenses become faster and faster, middle blocking is more and more difficult. Especially with our young middles on my varsity, we often send them out to the opponent's ace OH while our LF blocks middle and/or "chases" the 5 (backset). Rather than middles executing a weak block on both pins, we want a good block on one pin and no block on the other. For us, "A bad block is worse than no block." Finally, when a middle doesn't block, she is responsible for flowing to the play to pick up tips.

Once you begin to encounter opponents with multiple terminating attackers, it will be time to "go traditional" and employ a more popular defensive system, predicated on putting "four hands" (two blockers) in front of every attack. Until then, have some fun experimenting with limited blockers.

TIP 50: DON'T FORGET ABOUT COVERAGE

I'm a hypocrite.

I always tell my team that every point is worth the same on the scoreboard, whether it's a straight down hammer that bounces off the rafters or a miss-hit that dribbles off the block.

However, I actually believe these two kinds of points do carry more weight:

1. The "terminating" attack that has the offense beginning to celebrate but is miraculously dug by a defender.
2. The straight down block that is covered and then leads to a point.

These are the plays that can rip the heart out of a team, because just when they are ready to begin a massive celebration, it becomes apparent that the ball is still alive. Losing the point adds insult to injury.

Of the two situations, the coverage play might be the most devastating, since stuff blocks are so rare. Great coverage also allows your attackers to swing freely and know that if they are blocked, the coverage will be rock solid.

Now that I've convinced you of a cover play's importance, here are six keys to creating a successful coverage system:

1. **Put someone in charge of the communication.** Whether it's your libero or another back row position, having

someone responsible for calling, "Cover, cover!" will help your team be more attentive.

2. **Allow your team to cover any balls attacked into the net in practice.** This will give them far more opportunities to practice diligent coverage.

3. **Focus on E and P – "Eyes and Posture."** We want the eyes on the blockers' hands and the posture to be athletic and ready.

4. **Be sure the attacker covers, too.** Blocked balls will be coverable by the attacker 25-30% of the time. The attacker must land balanced and ready to self-cover.

5. **Review both transition coverage and serve-receive coverage.** These are not the same. Transition coverage doesn't change since your players will be coming from the same defensive positions. Serve-receive presents a more challenging situation. If your libero is positioned in RB in serve-receive, should she cover the first attack as an RB, or should she sprint to her LB position to cover? If she does sprint, will she be in the way of a back row pipe attack? Different coaches handle this issue in different ways; what's important is that you develop a coordinated system.

6. **Cover "high."** Getting the ball high in the air when covering will give your hitters time to transition to attack.

There you have it. Now you can prepare your squad to rip the heart out of your opponents with a bevy of coverage transition points.

TIP 51: STEAL MY FAVORITE SYSTEM FOR DEVELOPING TEAMS

I referred to much of this in Tip #42, but it's here in simplified form. If you are coaching a young and/or inexperienced team that should not yet be blocking, it's the ideal system for a couple of reasons. First, it's easy to teach and easy to learn; I can usually install all of it in one practice. Switches are also kept to a minimum, and this is a big plus for players learning to switch for the first time. Secondly, it allows your best players to explore their talents as both setters, attackers and defenders, and does this without using a back row setter in serve-receive or attack-transition. It also provides opportunities for every player to learn to hit from both the left and the right and to play all three back row positions.

Here's how it works:

1. Serve-receive and defense will be almost identical. The team will be in a 5-person W formation with the setter in MF five feet from the net. In SR, the middle back will be 18 feet from the net; on defense, she'll move up to 13 or 14 feet.

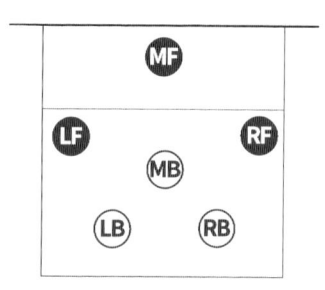

2. It's a 6-3 offense with the setter in MF. The 3 setters will be separated in the rotation, and each of them will attack when in LF and set when in MF and RF. In this situation, there is no switching at all in three rotations. In the other three, there's a simple switch of MF moving to hit on the right, so the RF setter (in the rotation) can move to her MF position.

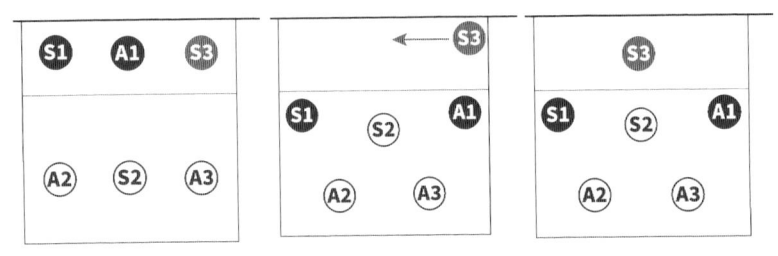

S3 is the current setter, S1 hits when in LF

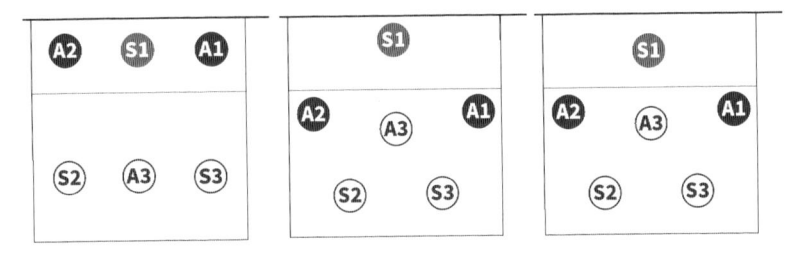

S1 is the current setter

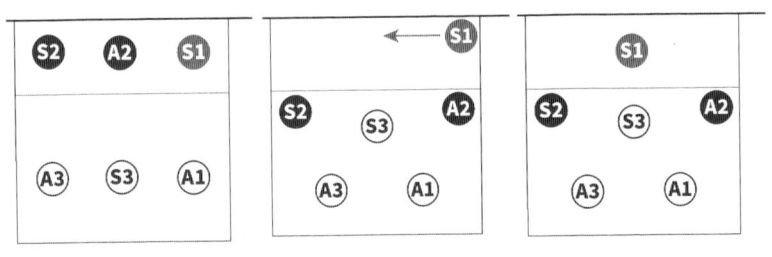

S1 is the current setter, S2 hits when in LF

121

3. I like to put my three best athletes in the setter positions. If one is not proficient enough with her hands, bump-setting will suffice at the start. The three will quickly discern that they are in the middle of the action, and because they are allowed to attack in LF, I don't get much pushback.

4. On tight sets, the front row setters always have the dump option available, and if they haven't learned to backset, they can simply turn and face either the LF or RF hitter.

5. If you want to expose the team to a back row setter with three attackers, I suggest installing it later in the season and doing it only on free balls. When this is installed, your players will again have a single, simple back row switch in only three rotations. In three rotations, a setter will already be playing RB. In the other three, she will switch with middle back. In the back row now, your three setters will set (FREE BALLS ONLY) when playing RB and middle back, and defend when playing LB.

We started this section with Robin Sharma, and we'll end with him. It's all about simplicity!

PART 6:
WHAT DO I DO DURING A MATCH?

TIP 52: PLAN AHEAD

There's nothing worse for a coach than becoming frazzled in the middle of a match. Your anxiety can not only damage your team's psyche, it can give your opponent confidence. The best prevention mechanism is a consistent pre-planning routine.

This seems so simple, but it took me several years of coaching to grasp the concept of disciplined preparation before a match. My first task in pre-planning is to create a "cheat sheet." This is a single piece of paper where I list my roster along with a whole host of different lineups, beginning with my favorite starting lineup and including that same lineup in all six rotations. This makes it super simple to "spin the wheel" if I want to create different matchups with the opposition. In this first series, I also include my normal sub patterns.

Rotation 1

Rotation 2

Rotation 3

Rotation 4

Rotation 5

Rotation 6

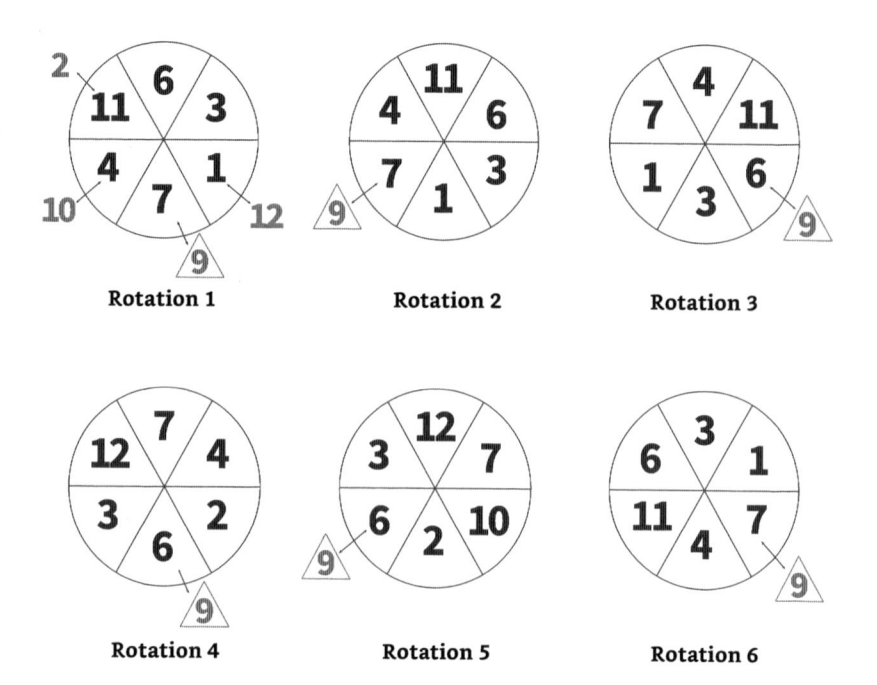

The second series of line-ups are contingencies if something unexpected happens. I'll imagine that each starter gets injured in the middle of a set and has to be replaced. It's important to have both a mid-set remedy as well as a solution for a new lineup for the next set. This can be quite simple; maybe you insert a sub mid-game and then start that same sub in the next one.

Part 6: What Do I Do During a Match?

On the other hand, it could be more involved, and perhaps between sets you'll have to make a system remedy – for instance, 6-2 to 5-1 – or change players' positions in order to field your best lineup.

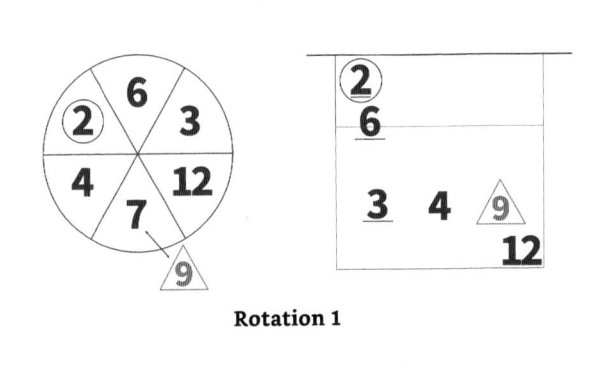

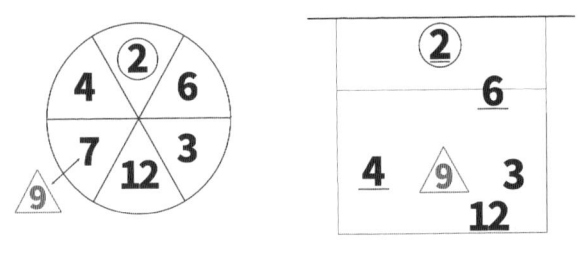

Rotation 1

Rotation 2

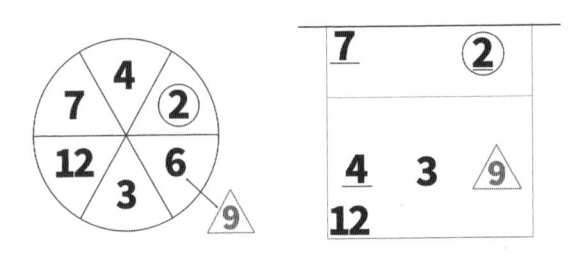

Rotation 3

125

So You Want to Be a Great Volleyball Coach

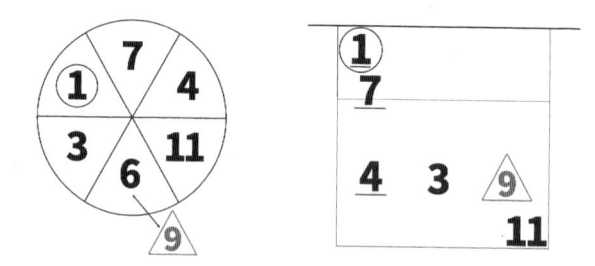

Rotation 4

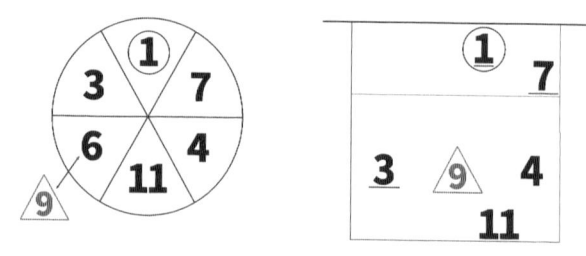

Rotation 5

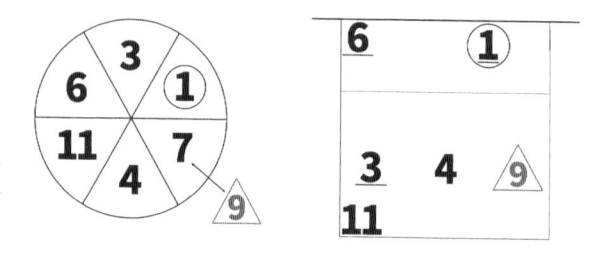

Rotation 6

126

Part 6: What Do I Do During a Match?

My third series of lineups are those I use when I need to make an adjustment. If we are down 0-2, it's important that I have lineup solutions ready and that I can communicate them with clarity. Maybe I want to flip-flop my two OH's or MA's, or perhaps I want to move my setter to OH and insert a different setter. Whatever the case may be, I want to be prepared.

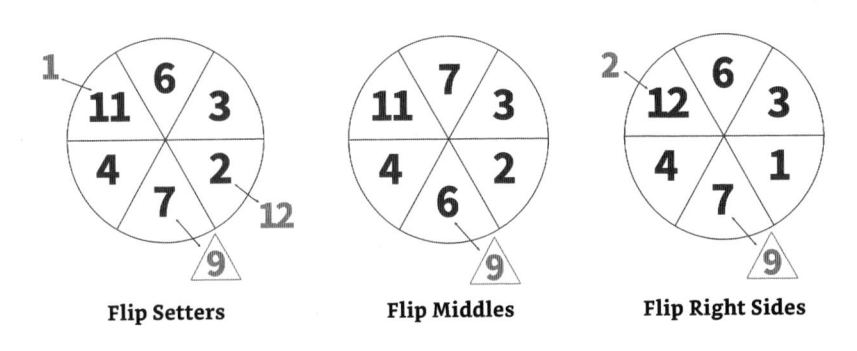

Flip Setters   **Flip Middles**   **Flip Right Sides**

In this last series, I also include lineups for situations when we may be far ahead. In those instances, I want to ensure that my substitutes get as much quality playing time as possible.

At the top of my cheat sheet, I write my roster twice – once with player names and numbers, and again with players listed by position. Having these clearly laid out helps me when I'm writing lineups and also when I'm making mid-game changes.

Players by name and number:

1. Maggie
2. Joy
3. Devin

4. Mary
5. Sophia
6. Angie
7. Lauren
8. Athena
9. Sara
10. Ally
11. Paula
12. Anna

Players by position:

- Setters: 1, 2 (12)
- Outsides: 3, 4, 5
- Middles: 6, 7, 8
- DS/Liberos: 9, 10
- Right Sides: 11, 12

Here's an example of what my cheat sheet looks like:

Part 6: What Do I Do During a Match?

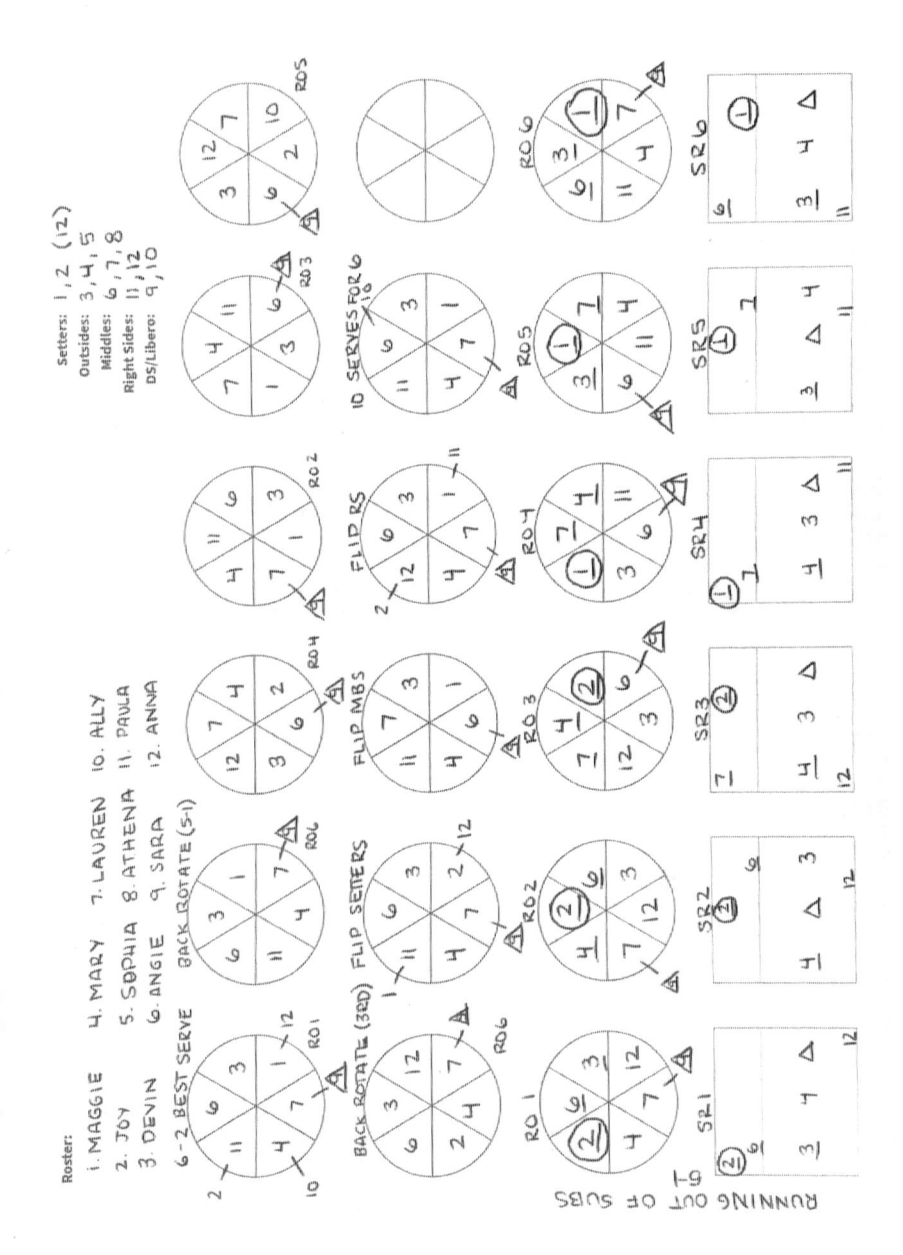

After my cheat sheet, my next task is to create a routine for writing the lineup and sharing it with my team. This might seem a bit elementary, but it's necessary. Take it from a guy who has made stupid lineup errors and then run around like a demon trying to put players in the proper positions. My routine involves first writing my lineup on the game-sheet that I carry in my notebook. Next, I transcribe this lineup onto the official card, double check it, and then hand it to the ref. My game-sheet lineup is on a volleyball rotation wheel. That way, before each game begins, I simply show my team the wheel, and they can see their starting positions.

My final task for this pre-planning tip is scouting. For my high school varsity, we might already have a scouting report, so I simply write our top three priorities on top of my game-sheet. If we haven't seen a team before (first match of a tournament), I might ask, "What did you see in warmups?" From our players' responses and my observation, we'll put together three priorities for the beginning of the match.

For my middle school team, we usually focus on serving and passing. Simply, we identify our opponent's best servers, as well as their location tendencies. For serve-receive, we try to identify strong passers we want to avoid serving. I'm not sure how meaningful this information is for our young players, but I do believe there's comfort in routine. If this pre-game scout chat gives even one player a bit more confidence, then it's worth it.

There are two more tasks in match preparation, but subbing and statting deserve their own tips.

TIP 53: KNOW YOUR GREATEST CHALLENGE

For the past 25 years, I've coached a talented high school varsity team in the fall, then run a developmental 12- and 14-under group in the winter and spring. On varsity, I usually carry 14 players. I try to limit the club teams to 10-11. Given those numbers, you'd think that subbing on varsity would be more difficult, but it isn't. Subbing on the club teams is far more challenging.

Here's why. Our varsity practices daily, competes in over 30 matches per season and, as one of the more talented teams in our county, we play to win. I clearly define roles, and players 11-14 know that they will rarely play in our most competitive matches. Because we work every day in practice to develop the skills of our non-starters, we don't use matches for their development. This clarity makes subbing relatively simple, and problems with players and families are rare.

On the other hand, our club teams practice only two days a week and compete in a total of six tournaments. The club players are younger, less experienced, and they need match play to learn and grow. Our model must be more developmental in nature. However, we are still keeping score, and winning is still more fun than losing. Now it should be clear why subbing on developmental teams is so challenging; balancing development with winning might be the hardest part of the job!

The easy way out of this dilemma is to operate on the extremes. You can designate your 12-under team as "elite," and you can run it like my high school varsity. There are obvious problems with this. How many 12-year-olds were ecstatic when they first made the "elite" team, then completely disheartened when they sat on the bench for 90% of their tournaments?

You can also swing hard to the developmental side and play everyone exactly the same amount of time. With a 12-person team, some coaches choose to play six players in the first set and the next six in the second. Often you can hear these coaches muttering after a loss, "If I played my best players as much as the other team, we would have won."

For me, there had to be a better way to tackle this difficult challenge. There had to be a way to keep my most talented players involved, develop our most inexperienced athletes, and teach and reinforce competitiveness. Here's what I developed over the years. Let's call it Subbing for Success.

TIP 54: SUB FOR SUCCESS

In trying to create a successful substitution model, I had to find a middle ground between the developmental and the competitive paradigms. I needed a more nuanced approach, but also one that would keep my competitive nature – overly competitive? – in check. I started by establishing clear guidelines that would help coaches, players and parents understand the method to our madness. They are:

- Every player will play between 40-90% of the time in matches.
- Every player will play in every set (even if it's for one play) and will start in at least two sets in every tourney.

(Our schedule was always the same – three best-of-three matches and no playoffs.)

- Coaches will put players in positions where they will be most successful. If a player has never served a ball over the net in practice, that player will not serve in the match.
- As the season progresses, the least experienced players get more playing time, not less.
- Between matches, coaches spend time giving "mini private lessons" to their most inexperienced players. Both players and parents notice that though these kids might be playing less than the most talented players, their development is a priority.

These criteria provided some flexibility when it came to subbing, and I needed it. Because our club is small, and we make no cuts, we often have huge talent gaps between our strongest and weakest players. Early in the season, I sub the raw beginners in quick spurts to help them learn. My experienced players stay on the court for longer stretches and are responsible for helping the newbies adapt.

Before I share my subbing formulas, I should mention one huge advantage that not everyone enjoys. Our league allows unlimited subbing, so it gives me great leeway to sub at will. Here are a few techniques I have employed:

- Two players share a position, one in the front row and one in the back row. They alternate serving.
- Two players share a position, but they do it by score. We can sub when the first team scores 13 (half a game)

or every time the high score hits a multiple of 5, 6 or 7. These are automatic subs made by the players, and if the sub isn't paying attention, she doesn't go in.

- Three players share a position, and they enter when the score hits 8 and 16. No player can be in a 3-player platoon for two consecutive sets.
- Two or three players share a position, and I make decisions during the set.

If you remember Tip #52, you know that it's all about preparation. I do a bunch of prep work on lineups the night before a tourney. After ranking players 1-11, strongest to weakest, this is my first set plan:

- Setters are 1, 2 and 3 – 1 and 2 play the entire set, and 3 will play front row and sub out in the back row with 9.
- 4 will serve and play back row, and 11 will play front row.
- 5 will play the first half of the set, and 6 will go in when the score hits 13.
- 7, 8 and 10 will be on a 3-player platoon; 10 will start and play until a team scores the 8th point, 8 will sub in and stay until the 16th point is scored, and then 7 will finish the set.

In the second set, 1 and 3 will be the "glue," and 2 will sub out of the back row; 7, 8, and 10 have to move to a two-player platoon. Of course, I reserve the right to flip-flop players at any time, and I will often take a player out for one play to teach a concept and put her right back in to try it. Because of my pre-planning, in-game subbing is relatively simple, since the players already have "slots." There's only one place in the lineup for each player to go, and they (and I) know that place before the set begins.

This system has helped me successfully balance developing our players and trying to win. Give it a go!

TIP 55: DETERMINE WHAT'S IMPORTANT AND STAT IT

Before retiring from the classroom in 2017, I was an English teacher. Though I always leaned more toward words than numbers, one of my favorite quotations is numerical in nature. It is, "What gets measured gets done." This always helped me as a teacher when I wanted to shape my students' behavior. If they weren't doing homework, I might increase its value in my grading system.

I also use this concept in coaching. Whatever statistic I choose to track helps shape the behavior of our players. Some coaches won't stat players in their developmental stages, but I think it's important to teach all players what is important and what to prioritize.

For our most inexperienced teams, I usually keep one statistic – serves in a row. It's a simple stat to take, and it's one that allows players to see their improvement. We celebrate whenever a player achieves her personal best, and also when a player sets a team record high. Once players get into the 20s, we usually raise the bar and only count serves that are antenna-high or lower. If I have the resources, the second stat I take for lower-level teams is ace prevention, which is passes in a row without getting aced. Once again, we can celebrate both personal bests and team record highs.

As the level of play improves, I usually add *attacking efficiency* to the mix. I explored this in depth in Tip #46, so I won't spend too much time on it here. The simple takeaway is that as soon as your team can consistently keep your opponents' ace percentage below 20%, *attacking efficiency* will be the most important metric when it comes to winning and losing.

Of course, deciding what to prioritize and stat is just the first step. You also have to find a way to keep the stats and ensure that they are as accurate as possible. Because I usually have my hands full with my subbing responsibilities, I normally have an assistant coach take stats. For developing teams, I don't mind using parents since the serves-in-a-row stat is fairly straightforward. On the other hand, I don't like to use players; I want them to be paying attention to the match, learning from players' successes and failures, and supporting their teammates.

OK. Enough of the pre-match stuff. Let's blow the whistle and get the game started.

TIP 56: STAY OUT OF THE PAST

When I was a young coach, I spent the majority of time in matches engaged in error correction. If a player hit a ball into the net, I would instruct her how to make a technique change so it would not happen again. I did the same thing after serving or passing errors. It was non-stop. Now, I cringe every time I think about this. I'm sure I did far more harm than good.

Here's why. Volleyball is a game of errors. Our players are battling gravity, and it's an unfair fight they are going to lose. After errors, the whistle blows, and everyone looks at them. That isn't the time for me to start blabbing about technique. It's a time for them to connect with their teammates in the huddle, "flush" the error and prepare for the next point. Furthermore, if you've done a decent job in practice, your players should know why they made the error. The last thing they need after a mistake is for you to "rub it in" with some "instruction."

So now that I'm no longer an error-corrector, what do I do? Good question. Instead of an error corrector, I'm a catcher of good stuff, a predictor, and a reminder. As it relates to errors, I try to stay out of the past as much as possible. However, I will go there to catch players doing good stuff that others might overlook. For example, if we set our top attacker for a thundering kill, I might celebrate the pass, the set or the players who covered. The attacker gets plenty of positive feedback; she doesn't need anything from me.

As a cagey veteran, most of my communication during a match is now future-focused. Here are a few examples:

- "Let's be ready for the overpass." (As our best server goes back to serve.)
- "Know their blockers here." (To our setter and attackers when their weakest blocker reaches the front row.)
- "This server likes to serve short."

- "Front row setter likes to dump in this rotation."
- "Let's get every offspeed here." (After we have a stuff block.)
- "Yes, Jackie. That's just what I was thinking." (After Jackie says one of the above.)

By getting out of the past and into the future, I provide a good model for our players. If I want them to be next-play focused, then I need to be there as well.

Of course, by now you know me, and if you are skeptical that I could completely give up error-correction, you are right. I still error-correct a bit, but I have one rule to follow, and it's a simple one. I can only error-correct after we WIN a point. After we score a point, players are in a much better frame of mind to take instruction. If I say, "Angie, don't forget to cover" or "Mary, I think you have time to close the block there," since the errors didn't cost us points, the instructions are taken more as reminders than criticisms.

I hope you can play around with a couple of these concepts. One thing I know for sure, I have much more fun coaching now than I did when I was a young whippersnapper.

TIP 57: BE A GRACIOUS WINNER AND A GRATEFUL LOSER

In the previous tip, I explained how my approach to coaching in matches has evolved considerably, and so has my take on winning and losing. As a young coach consumed by competitive angst, I was giddy after wins and dejected after losses.

I viewed each competition as the ultimate test of my coaching abilities, and there were no grades in the middle; it was either an "A" or an "F." When we won, I remembered every great play, and all our players were "clutch." When we lost, I only remembered the errors, and all our players "choked under pressure."

As I've "grown older" (my wife won't let me use "matured"), the wins and losses look a bit different. Now, I have a more balanced perspective on competition that is process-oriented rather than product-oriented. Instead of chasing wins, I simply ask my team to use every competition as an opportunity to improve.

Using this paradigm, I now frame wins much differently than I did early in my career. Rather than basking in the glow of victory, I'm more focused on identifying the specific areas that we improved and how those influenced the positive result. There will also be rare situations (hopefully) when we win but don't really improve. I will be straightforward and honest with the team, and the message will be clear; it's not all about winning. Though winning is fun, and we always do all we can to pursue it, it's more important that we improve, both in our play and our togetherness as a team.

My response to losses is even more different than in my early days. Now, we frame the losses as an important part of our growth. They teach us how to deal with adversity, and they help us better identify our strengths and weaknesses. I am grateful for what these teach me as a coach, and they only strengthen my resolve to help the team continue to improve.

Of course, our players (and parents) might still be hyper-focused on winning and losing, and that's OK. The scoreboard is a powerful attraction, and my emphasis on growth will not change that. However, it will keep my team on more of an even keel. I will always teach and reinforce competitiveness, but by making improvement a priority, I can avoid the high highs and low lows that were the trademark of my teams of yesteryear.

Finally, the growth paradigm helps me better prepare my team for any kind of match. There's a comforting consistency in our focus to improve. Whether we are playing a team considerably stronger or one considerably weaker, we want to gather at the end of both matches, filled with pride, stating, "We are better at volleyball, and we are more together as a team than we were two hours ago."

TIP 58: LEARN FROM MY POST-MATCH DEBACLE

Recently, I was asked this question at a clinic, "What's the worst mistake you've made in your career?" Easy answer. It was a post-match speech I gave my high school team back in the late 1990s.

Here is the scene. It was early season on a Tuesday. We had just won a tournament on the previous Saturday, so we were feeling a bit full of ourselves, me included. We were preparing to play our neighborhood rival at their gym. As I observed our team in warmups, we looked casual and careless. I said nothing.

We started the match slowly, and I thought our bench was quiet and scattered. Again, I said nothing at the time. The match seesawed back and forth, and we ended up losing a nail-biter 17-15 in the fifth. In that deciding set, we lost two crucial points on simple communication errors.

Post-match I was livid, and I tore into the team. I made a bunch of references to "no heart," and every player on the team was targeted. I ripped our captains, our seniors, our starters, and our subs. Everyone was to blame, except me of course. I took no responsibility.

The result of this nonsense was predictable. I completely lost the trust of the team, and I struggled to connect for the rest of the uneventful season. The lessons here are simple but important:

- **Give immediate feedback:** If I didn't like the way the warmup looked, I should have immediately stopped it and asked, "Is this our best focus right now? Let's do a little better." Instead, I said nothing and let my frustration fester.

- **Use time-outs to address our values:** Likewise, I should have called a time-out and asked all of our players, "Are we giving everything we can to each other right now? Whether you are on the floor or on the bench, can we make it look and sound more like it did at the end of the tourney? I'll be better, too." Again, I said nothing, and only became more irritated.

- **Focus on communication:** Whenever things are a bit wonky, it's always good to reinforce player communication. Communication is completely under our control, and it can help both our play and our togetherness. Of course, I never asked the team to make this a priority.

- **Take responsibility:** If any person needed to be "ripped" after the match, it was the head coach. The team wasn't prepared to play, and that is my responsibility. Any negative feedback to the team should have started with my errors.

- **Establish a routine so you avoid emotional stupidity:** It seems obvious that addressing the team after an emotional loss can be fraught with peril. But because I hadn't established a consistent post-match routine, I fell victim to the temptation to immediately "fix" our problems.

The best thing about this mistake is that I never made it again. It forced me to develop an end-of-match routine that I continue to use to this day. Every player shares one example she observed during the match of a teammate modeling great effort, teamness or attitude. We are not looking for highlight plays; we are looking to recognize all the little glue that holds teams together. After each player takes a turn, each coach will. Once our values are positively reinforced, we do a cheer and leave.

So no more speeches. We can deal with areas to improve in the next practice.

TIP 59: FIND A COUPLE OF IDIOTS

I have nothing against mentors. In fact, I'm extremely fortunate to have started my career working with two coaching legends in San Diego, Digger Graybill and Hal Mitrovich. How lucky was I to begin my coaching journey with these two masters! They both made it look so easy; they taught with such care and clarity, and their players played so hard. I was in the gym with them every day, soaking up an endless amount of coaching wisdom.

Though their influence was substantial, especially in the early stages of my career, I could argue that a couple of other "idiots" had just as much impact on my development as a coach. I use "idiot" as a term of endearment, as I am a proud member of the group. The moniker is also an acknowledgement to my wife (and the other spouses) who had to put up with non-stop volleytalk from the idiots at every social event. It got so bad that the spouses collaborated to establish "VB moratoriums," designated times when we were prohibited from talking shop.

The idiots were different from the mentors because we were all a long way from mastering anything. Yet we shared a passion for the game, and we were coaching non-stop. It was a fertile learning environment. With the idiots, no idea was too stupid, and we could immediately test it out in the gym, and then report back to the group. Sharing our daily challenges also helped accelerate our learning. At the time, I was not only coaching my team, but I was also closely connected to the successes and failures of all the teams in our coaching circle.

It's no surprise to me that our merry band of idiots has done quite well in the profession. Josh is an outstanding Division I coach, and Ozhan runs one of the most successful clubs in the country. DJ continues to coach with me and is among the most talented and beloved teachers/coaches at our school.

If you can work with a mentor or two, that's great. I'm all for it. But it's equally important to find your own band of passionate coaching colleagues who will be there right beside you, bumbling and stumbling toward success.

TIP 60: SHARPEN YOUR EAVESDROPPING SKILLS

It took me a while to get the hang of being an eavesdropper. I was a bit self-conscious at first, but as I became more comfortable closely observing and listening to accomplished coaches, the benefits were too great. I learned too much, and any hesitation disappeared.

Here is my strategy. First, it's difficult to do at a high school or college match because it's tougher to blend in. But tournaments are the perfect forum. Whether I'm coaching at the tournament or there to spectate, I always like to arrive early to watch warmups, and I'm immediately on the lookout for teams that are using this time most efficiently. When matches begin, though the most talented teams attract the most eyes, I'm more interested in the teams that seem to "punch above their weight." These are the teams that appear to be overmatched in the warmup but end up fairing far better than you'd expect against a more physical or more talented opponent.

Once I identify a target, I will spend as much time as I can watching the team play. I choose a place to observe that is as close to the coach as possible. I want to hear everything the coach has to say, both to players and to other coaches. During time-outs, I lean in to hear what little nugget I might be able to steal.

Occasionally, I have to contend with testy parents who believe I am trying to gain some advantage that I will exploit when our teams play. Their cold glares and snide remarks rarely deter me. If I'm adding to my coaching toolbox, I'm happy. Here is a short list of what I look for when I target a master coach:

- Does the coach see things that I don't see?
- What does the coach celebrate?
- When and how does the coach give feedback?
- Does the coach prioritize things that I don't prioritize?
- How does the coach respond to winning and losing?

The most important takeaway from all my years of eavesdropping is that there's no single formula for successfully coaching volleyball. There are countless ways to get the job done, and that's what makes coaching so fun and challenging. There is always more I can learn and always room for improvement.

TIP 61: KEEP YOUR EYE OFF THE BALL

One of the ways to hone your skills as a coach is to watch a ton of volleyball. Whether it's live play or video, there are always lessons to be learned observing your own team, your opponents, or college and professional teams.

There's one bit of magic to watching volleyball that I learned far too late in my career. *Keep your eye **off** the ball.* The ball is mesmerizing, and it's always tempting to track it and watch the game as a fan. However, the master coach is adept at resisting the urge to "ball watch" and to instead focus on player perception and movement.

Of course, the central question is, "If I'm not watching the ball, what exactly should I watch?" Here is a short list that might help break the "ball watching" habit:

1. **Transition:** Watch your attackers after they block or defend and see how they transition and prepare to hit. Do they run out of "the box" (the rectangle formed by the 10-foot line, sidelines and center line) or are they shuffling their feet inside the box?

2. **SR passing perception and movement:** Are passers moving before the ball reaches the net, or do they wait until the ball crosses the plane before they prepare to pass?

3. **Attacker timing:** We have specific footwork timing for fast in-system sets and slow out-of-system sets. In most in-system situations, our pin attackers should be on their second (or left) step in their four-step approach on setter contact. Out-of-system, they should be balanced and not moving on setter contact.

4. **Blockers:** Are blockers picking up cues to choose the best spots to block? Are their hands taking some area, or are they too close together?

5. **Setter penetration:** Is the setter sprinting to the target area so she is stopped and balanced on passer contact?
6. **Setter decision making:** Does the setter know the capabilities and tendencies of the opponent's middle blocker? Specifically, is the middle blocker committing on the quick attack, releasing to "trap" a dominant pin hitter, or is she reading?
7. **Floor defenders:** Are they picking up cues from the set location and the attacker, then adjusting their positions accordingly? Are they balanced and ready to move?
8. **Coverage:** Are players in posture and covering with intent?

This is by no means a complete list, but it should get you started. Not only will it help you to better dissect the game, you can then teach your players how to do it as well.

TIP 62: STAY CURIOUS

As I mentioned way back in Tip #1, the best coaches share a common trait – curiosity. They are always looking for ways to sharpen their skills and improve their craft. Given that you have reached the final tip, you are in the club. I hope this book satisfied a bit of your curiosity and provided some useful coaching nuggets.

Of course, it doesn't end here. There's so much great coaching material out there, and it's more accessible than ever. When I first started coaching, the biggest problem was finding any quality volleyball coaching material. Now the biggest challenge is sifting through the reams of information to discover the very best.

Here's quick look at six of my favorites sources:

- **The Art of Coaching Volleyball website:** I'm more than a little biased here, but I love the variety of information on the site. Every time I start to browse, I'm always amazed at the new material I discover.
  www.theartofcoachingvolleyball.com

- **Coach Your Brains Out podcast:** These guys are all coaches, and I've picked up all sorts of great tidbits from their pod.
  www.blog.goldmedalsquared.com/podcast

- **Volleyball Coaches and Trainers Facebook group:** I'm not a savvy social media guy, but this group is a fun one. They constantly explore common coaching challenges, and they have a sweet little PDF resource library.
  www.facebook.com/groups/volleycoaches

- **The VolleyNerd podcast:** Once again, this is a definite homer recommendation. Davis Ransom is one of San Diego's top coaches, and the kid's got some talent behind the mic as well!
  www.anchor.fm/davis-ransom

- **The Little Book of Talent by Daniel Coyle:** My favorite coaching book, and when you check out the book's format, you won't be too surprised why I like it so much.
  www.danielcoyle.com/little-book-talent

- **Coaching DNA podcast:** Yet another pod, but this one is a bit more generic. Travis Wycoff is the host, and he's a former baseball guy who recently interviewed a bunch of volleyball coaches.
  www.kingdomcoachingtw.com/podcast

Of course, this list is a mere drop in the bucket. It doesn't even get into my video addiction and the number of hours I spend on YouTube and Hudl.

Good luck with your coaching journey! If you have questions, comments, feedback, complaints, don't hesitate to contact me at mattoxt@theartofcoaching.com.

Take care,
Tod

ABOUT THE AUTHOR

Tod Mattox has been coaching volleyball in San Diego since 1982, working extensively with high school and club girls' programs. In addition, he has coached boys' high school, AVP women and a bit of men's college. Tod recently retired from his "real job" – teaching English at The Bishop's School in La Jolla. He continues to coach at Bishop's and recently completed his 25th year heading the girls' varsity team. Until 2019, Tod was the owner/director/head coach of a small local volleyball club that served inexperienced 12- and 14-unders. After selling the club, he began his current work in coaches' education with The Art of Coaching Volleyball and Coast Volleyball Club. Tod is a current board member and long-time supporter of Starlings Volleyball, USA, a non-profit that serves at-risk girls.